NOTES ON ASSAYING

AND

ASSAY SCHEMES;

BY

PIERRE DE PEYSTER RICKETTS, E. M., PH. D.
Instructor, in charge of the Assay Laboratory of the
School of Mines, Columbia College.

NEW YORK:
THE ART PRINTING ESTABLISHMENT, 30 BOND STREET.
1876.

CONTENTS.

PART FIRST.

Introduction.
Balances and Weights.
Furnaces and Fuels.
Crucibles, Scorifiers, and Cupels.
Lutes, Cements, and Washes.
Fixtures, Tools, and Apparatus.
Reagents and Chemicals.
Preliminary Testing of Ores.
Sampling and Pulverizing.
Weighing Ore and Reagents.
Calcination and Roasting.
Reduction and Fusion.
Distillation and Sublimation.
Scorification and Cupellation.
Inquartation and Parting.
Weighing Buttons and Bullion.
Tabulating Results and Reporting.

PART SECOND.

Assay of Lead.
" " Antimony.
" " Gold and Silver.
" " Platinum.
" " Zinc.
" " Mercury.
" " Bismuth.
" " Tin.
" " Copper.
" " Iron.
" " Nickel and Cobalt.
" " Carbon.

PART THIRD.

PART FOURTH.

APPENDIX.

Manipulation, Formulæ, and Calculation.

Blowpipe Analysis, Apparatus, and Reagents.

Chemical Apparatus and Reagents.

Scheme for Qualitative Analysis.—Zettnow.

ERRATA.

Page.	Line.	
39	14	For "($C_{12}H_{22}O_{11}$) Sugar," read, *Sugar* ($C_{12}H_{22}O_{11}$),
44	Bottom	For "page 28" read, *page* 32
59	7	For "sufficiently abundant to acquire" read, *in sufficient abundance to have*
62	13 from bottom.	For "amount of arsenic," read, *amount of sulphur, arsenic,*
135	7	For "67.4" read, 77.4
135	3 from bottom.	For "20 grains" read, 24 *grains*
138	8 from bottom.	For "soluble or insoluble." read, *and is insoluble.*
141	Bottom	Example should read: 4134 2067 16536 12402 ——— $4518.462
159	12	For "Sp. Ph." read, *S. Ph.*

PREFACE.

In preparing this little manual I have endeavored to meet two wants, and supply a book that will answer for the practical assayer and miner, as well as the scientific student; and although I know there is much room for criticism, I trust it will prove acceptable to both.

The work embodies the system of assaying practiced in the School of Mines of Columbia College, which has been organized and developed by Prof. C. F. Chandler and by G. M. Miller, E. C. H. Day, T. M. Blossom, E. M., and the author of these notes, who have successively had charge of the assay laboratory.

The parts on gold, silver, and iron are founded on the excellent papers published by Mr. Blossom, in the *American Chemist* for 1870—such modifications and additions having been made as were deemed necessary from experience. The table of silver and gold minerals, page 133, is given entire, as arranged by him.

Many of the methods given have been tested in the laboratory, and the results appended under the head of remarks, after each metal considered.

All chemical names have been avoided as far as possible, and where necessary, the old terms have been employed; the new with formulæ being given in parenthesis, and in the appendix for reference.

Much attention has been paid to the various processes and details peculiar to the West, and in this particular I have had the practical assistance of Mr. S. G. SACKETT; to whose pencil I am also indebted for most of the illustrations given. The furnace and desk drawings have been made sectional and to a scale; so as to serve as a guide in constructing the same.

A few hints on blowpipe analysis have been introduced in the appendix, as I have found that instrument an important aid in testing and assaying ores; also lists of blowpipe and analytical apparatus and reagents.

The advertisements in the back of the book, have been added for the purpose of furnishing a guide to those who wish to procure assay apparatus, chemicals, etc.

PIERRE DE P. RICKETTS.

ASSAY LABORATORY,
SCHOOL OF MINES,
June 1st, 1876.

PART I.

INTRODUCTION, APPARATUS, REAGENTS AND OPERATIONS.

INTRODUCTION.

Assaying has for its object the determination and extraction of the metallic elements from their various compounds.

The rules are empirical, and a knowledge of chemistry is not absolutely necessary, although the assayer will find that a familiarity with chemical laws and reactions will greatly facilitate his work. The following is a list of the elementary bodies as far as known, with their combining weights and symbols. An element is a body which chemical research has failed to reduce to a more simple form, or separate into constituent parts. The symbol of an element is the first letter or letters of its Latin name ; and its combining weight is the smallest number of units which will enter into combination with other elements; the first column of figures being the old and the second the new system of combining weights. Hydrogen is taken as unity in both systems.

TABLE OF ELEMENTS AND COMBINING WEIGHTS.

	OLD.	NEW.		OLD.	NEW.		OLD.	NEW.
Aluminum, ... Al...	13.7	27.4	*Gold,......... Au..	197.	197.	Rhodium,..... Ro...	52.2	104.4
*Antimony,... Sb...	122.	122.	Hydrogen,..... H...	1.	1.	Rubidium,.... Rb ..	85.4	85.4
Arsenic, ... As...	75.	75.	Indium,....... In...	56.7	113.4	Ruthenium,.. Ru...	52.2	104.4
Barium,....... Ba...	68.5	137.	Iodine,......... I...	127.	127.	Selenium, ... Se...	39.7	79.4
*Bismuth,...... Bi..	210.	210.	Iridium,....... Ir...	99.	198.	Silicon, ... Si...	14.	28.
Boron,......... B...	11.	11.	*Iron,......... Fe...	28.	56.	*Silver,....... Ag...	108.	108.
Bromine,...... Br...	80.	80.	Lanthanum,.. La...	46.	92.	Sodium,...... Na...	23.	23.
Cadmium,.... Cd...	56.	112.	*Lead,........ Pb...	103.5	207.	Strontium,.... Sr...	43.8	87.6
Cæsium, ... Cs...	133.	133.	Lithium,...... Li...	7.	7.	Sulphur,........ S...	16.	32.
Calcium,...... Ca...	20.	40.	Magnesium,.. Mg...	12.	24.	Tantalum,.... Ta...	182.	182.
*Carbon,....... C...	6.	12.	*Manganese,. Mn...	27.5	55.	Tellurium,.... Te...	64.	128.
Cerium, ... Ce...	46.	92.	*Mercury,.... Hg...	100.	200.	Thallium,..... Tl...	204.	204.
Chlorine,...... Cl...	35.5	35.5	Molybdenum, Mo..	48.	96.	Thorium, ... Th..	115.7	231.5
Chromium,.... Cr...	26.1	52.2	*Nickel, ... Ni...	29.4	58.8	*Tin,......... Sn...	59.	118.
*Cobalt,...... Co...	29.4	58.8	Nitrogen,...... N...	14.	14.	Titanium,..... Ti...	25.	50.
Columbium,.. Cb...	94.	94.	Osmium,...... Os...	99.6	199.2	Tungsten, ... W...	92.	184.
*Copper, ... Cu. .	31.7	63.4	Oxygen,........ O...	8.	16.	Uranium,...... U...	60.	120.
Didymium,.... D...	47.5	95.	Palladium,.... Pd...	53.3	106.6	Vanadium, . .. V...	51.3	51.3
Erbium,....... E...	56.3	112.6	Phosphorus,.... P...	31.	31.	Yttrium,....... Y...	30.8	61.7
Fluorine,...... F...	19.	19.	*Platinum,.... Pt...	98.7	197.4	*Zinc,......... Zn..	32.6	65.2
Glucinum,..... Gl...	46.	92.	Potassium,.... K...	39.1	39.1	Zirconium,.... Zr...	44.8	89.6

The names of the elements treated in the following pages are marked with an asterisk.

The combining weights or equivalents have been taken from the table prepared by Prof. CHANDLER, for the use of the students of the School of Mines; in which the latest values are given.

The various methods for the determination of the metals in their compounds may be classed under two heads:

1st. "Dry way," or assaying proper.

2d. "Wet way," or analysis.

The first includes all determinations by the direct action of heat, the various operations being performed in furnaces.

The second head embraces the estimation and separation of the elements by the action of solvents aided or unaided by heat, the use of furnaces not being essential.

There are many cases, of course, where the first class merges into the second, and *vice versa.*

It was originally intended to give in the following pages only a few concise methods for the estimation of the metals in their ores by fire assay; but, as in many ores the precious metals are associated with others which are either of value or detriment, and whose determination is often necessary, a few schemes for the treatment of such ores in the wet way have been added.

The various operations which may take place in making an assay proper, are—

1st. Preliminary testing of the ore.

2d. Preparation of the ore, sampling, pulverizing, etc.

3d. Weighing out the ore and reagents.

4th. Calcination and roasting.

5th. Reduction and fusion.

6th. Distillation and sublimation.

7th. Scorification and cupellation.

8th. Inquartation and parting, including solution.

9th. Weighing beads and bullion.

10th. Tabulating results and reporting.

All of the above will be described further on; but as some of the operations require great care in their performance, a few rules and hints for the guidance of the beginner may not be out of place.

1st. Sample well and carefully, for without a fair sample the assay is useless.

2d. Weigh carefully, and adjust the balance before weighing.

3d. Always weigh an ore before roasting, and roast thoroughly.

4th. Never fill a crucible or scorifier more than three-quarters full, and when a crucible is removed from the fire, tap it on the floor to settle the metal, unless otherwise directed, and keep the same covered.

5th. To break a crucible, hit with a middle-sized hammer near the centre, so as to break off the top at one blow. Then lay the bottom on the anvil, and crack it through to get the button whole. Never break until perfectly cold.

To break a scorifier, lay it bottom up on the anvil; encircle with the hand, and then strike the bottom. The button will generally come out free from slag.

6th. Never take a scorification or cupellation from the furnace to finish at a future time, but complete the operation at once. When buttons are scorified or cupelled, be sure that they are free from moisture.

7th. Be certain that all reagents used in an assay are dry and pure, especially when testing for the precious metals.

8th. In reporting results, recollect, that a fire assay does not always give the exact amount of metal contained, but often shows only what the yield of an ore would be in smelting, and that the assay of a small piece of ore can not represent the value of the bed or vein from which it may have been taken, and word your report accordingly.

9th. Always observe the color and character of the slag produced in an assay, as the nature of the ore treated may often be determined in this way.

BALANCES AND WEIGHTS.

Four balances will be found useful in an assay laboratory.

a.—A rough scales for weighing large samples of ores, metals, fluxes in bulk, &c. An ordinary grocer's scale will do very well.

b.—A balance for weighing out ore for assay, and the buttons of the base metals. (Fig. 1). This balance should

Fig. 1.

take ten ounces in each pan, turn with one-twentieth of a grain; and be provided with movable pans, level, and set-screws for adjusting. It is generally placed on a box, with drawer for weights.

c.—Hanging scales for fluxes. The pans made of horn, and supported by threads to a brass beam. It should carry at least ten ounces, and turn with one-half grain.

d.—The button or bullion scale, (Fig. 2). This balance should be used for nothing but gold and silver beads, or bullion; and must be accurate and extremely sensitive.

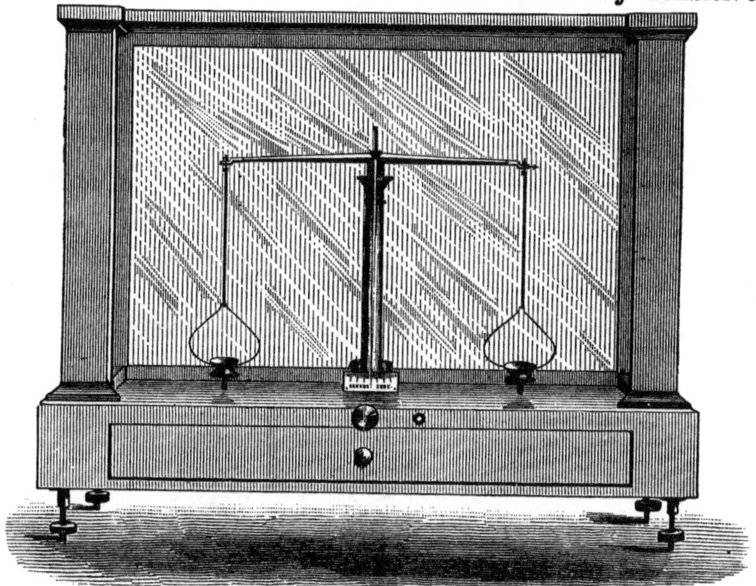

FIG. 2.

When loaded with one gramme, it should turn with one one-hundredth of a millegramme, and requires to be handled with the greatest care. It is provided with steel knives, agate bearings, spirit level, and set-screws.

To Adjust this Balance.—First turn the set-screws, two at a time, until the bubble is in the centre of the level, and the balance is firm. Then note the number of divisions the needle indicates on the scale when vibrated, counting from the second swing. If it shows equally on both sides of the centre line it is correct. Never leave the rest down, or raise it when the needle is not near the centre line, as the knife-edges are likely to be thrown off their bearings and the balance injured. To clean, an artist's blending-brush is very convenient, as it is soft and fine.

THE WEIGHTS employed by the assayer are—

a.—Avoirdupois for ores, base metals, and fluxes.

b.—Troy for gold, silver, &c.

c.—The French system based upon the gramme as a unit. These weights can be used for weighing ores, fluxes, and results; and will always be found convenient, as they are on the scale of ten.

d.—The assay weights, which is a system made up from a comparison of the three foregoing, will be found extremely simple and useful, saving a vast amount of calculation and labor (see table, page 136).

The unit of the system is the assay ton=29.166 grammes. Its derivation will be seen at a glance.

One lb. avoirdupois=7,000 Troy grains.

2,000 lbs.=one ton.

2,000×7,000=14,000,000 Troy grains, in one ton avoirdupois.

480 Troy grains=1 oz. Troy.

14,000,000÷480=29,166+Troy ozs. in 2,000 lbs. avoirdupois.

There are 29,166 millegrammes in one assay ton (A. T.); hence—

2,000 lbs. is to 1 A. T. as 1 oz. Troy is to 1 millegramme.

EXAMPLE.—Weigh an A. T. of ore, and if on assay it yields one millegramme of gold or silver, the result reads one Troy oz. in 2,000 lbs. avoirdupois, without further calculation.

Should the assayer desire to make quantitative determinations in the wet way, he will require, besides the above, an analytical balance, which will carry 100 grammes in each pan, and turn with one-twentieth of a millegramme. This balance should be provided with apparatus for taking specific gravities, rider, and weighing-tubes.

FURNACES AND FUELS.

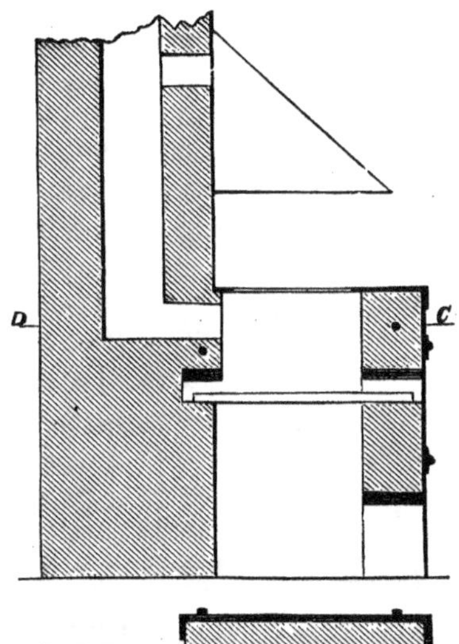

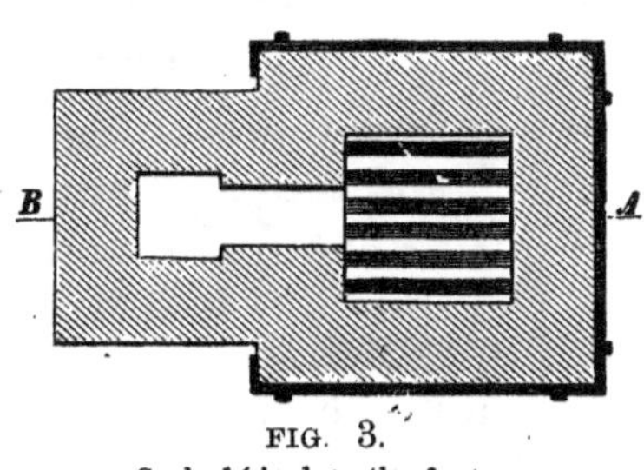

FIG. 3.
Scale ⅛-inch to the foot.

1st. FURNACE FOR CALCINING OR ROASTING.— Fig. 3 represents two sections.

The fireplace is made shallow; and, as a high temperature is not required, it may be made of red brick, or only lined with fire-brick, and the body of the furnace bound with strap-iron.

It should also have a cast-iron top-plate.

The grate-bars may be in one piece or separate, and draw out. The ash-pit should be provided with a door, which may be closed or opened in order to regulate the draft.

A hood of sheet-iron will also be found necessary in many cases, as the fumes given off in roasting are often injurious. It is an excellent plan to have the hood of galvanized iron to prevent rusting.

The chimney may be of brick, iron or clay.

2d. FURNACE FOR FUSION OR MELTING (Fig. 4).—This furnace should be deeper than the preceding one, and like it, may be built of red brick, but it is better to line it with fire brick.

For heavy work the furnace should be low, to facilitate

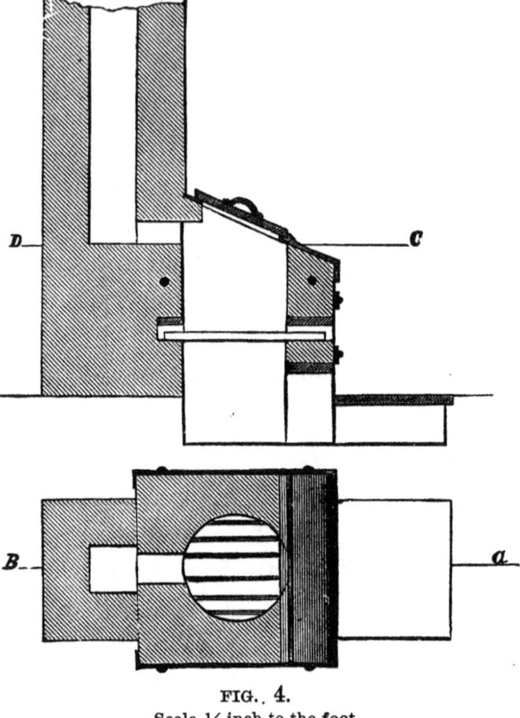

FIG. 4.
Scale ½-inch to the foot.

the lifting in and out of crucibles. Sometimes a crane is added for this purpose.

The chimney ought to be of brick, and the larger and higher it is, the stronger the draft. This may be regulated by a damper as well as by the ash-pit door.

The top should be of cast-iron, and the cover roll or slide easily.

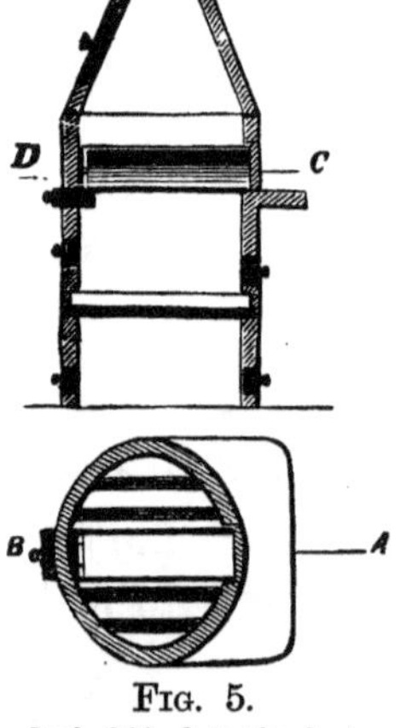

FIG. 5.
Scale ⅜-inch to the foot.

3d. MUFFLE FURNACE FOR SCORIFICATION AND CUPELLATION. Fig. 5 shows sections of a portable cupel furnace.

The same furnace may be used for both operations, but generally it will be found convenient to have a larger muffle for scorification and higher heat.

The muffles are made of refractory clay, and in one piece; and should be thoroughly dried before using.

The draft of the furnace ought to be sufficient to carry off fumes, which are often injurious. The construction of the furnace will vary with the fuel used and work to be done.

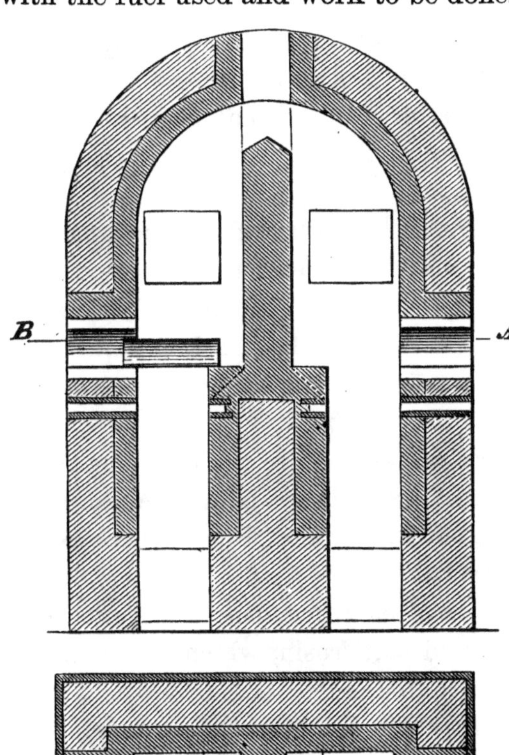

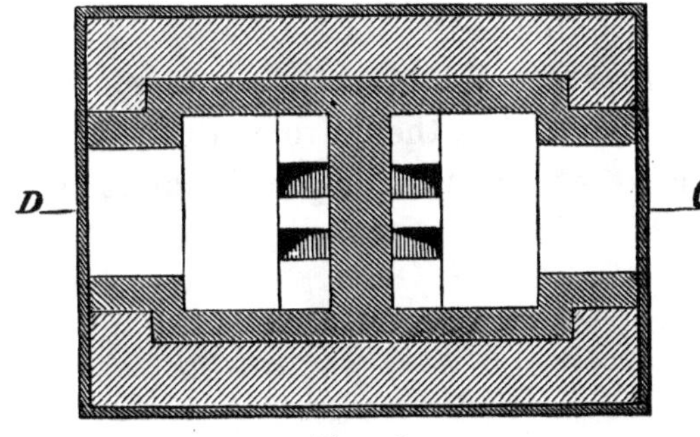

FIG. 6.
Scale ⅜-inch to the foot.

Fig. 6 shows the vertical and horizontal sections of a double muffle scorification furnace, for works where a large number of scorifications are required.

It has been in use in the assay laboratory of the School of Mines, New York, for two years, and its value has been proved. The muffles are larger than usual, and can be drawn out.

The whole furnace is lined with fire-brick, as is indicated by the fine shading.

By placing a damper at the top, one-half may be used to the exclusion of the other.

THE FUELS employed are coke, anthracite, bituminous

coal, and charcoal. Sometimes oil and gas are employed for small laboratory furnaces.

The coke should be about egg size and free from sulphur. It is chiefly used in calcining and fusion furnaces.

Charcoal, anthracite, and bituminous coal may be employed for the muffle furnace. The latter fuel requiring, however, a special furnace.

Anthracite coal, stove size, is best adapted for the assayer's purpose, but charcoal may be used as a substitute for either coke or anthracite, when it can be had more cheaply; it gives a hot fire, and is easily regulated; but requires constant attention, and the pieces used should be of medium size.

Various oil and gas furnaces are in use with varying results, but the limits of this work will not permit a description of them. See "Mitchell's Manual of Practical Assaying," pages 71 to 107 inclusive.

In lighting a fire it will be often convenient to use pieces of cork or corncobs saturated with rosin, which burn well, are cheap, and save much trouble.

To use, it is only necessary to light a piece and lay it upon a little kindling-wood placed in the bottom of the furnace, then put a few pieces of wood on top and add the coal.

CRUCIBLES.

A good crucible should stand sudden changes of temperature, be infusible, impermeable, and not attacked by fused substances.

The crucibles in use may be arranged in the following order.

1. Black lead, or graphite for melting.

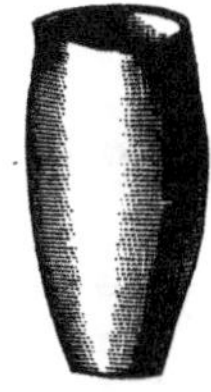

2. French clay. (Fig. 7.)

3. Hessian sand crucibles, round and triangular. (Fig. 8.)

FIG 7. FIG. 8.

4. Charcoal-lined crucibles.

The most refractory crucibles are cut out of quick lime, or can be moulded from magnesia, and chloride of magnesium, but the latter, however, are soft and not very strong.

The composition of the black lead crucibles is generally one part of refractory clay, to three of graphite; but sand is sometimes used. If the crucibles contain too much silicious matter they are liable to be acted upon by the melted charge, or the bases contained in the coal around them when in the fire.

These crucibles run in sizes from 1 to 400. The smallest holding from two to three pounds of metal. The next, four to six, and so on.

The demand is for two kinds, "steel" and "brass;" but they can be employed for melting all substances which are not oxydizing in their action.

French crucibles are made of Paris clay and fine sand, and rank among the best, but are more expensive than the Hessian. For melting charges which can be poured they are superior as the crucible can be used again. The sizes run from 1 to 20, with covers to match.

The composition of the ordinary Hessian crucible is about three-quarters clay (German), and one-quarter sand. They are round and triangular, and run in regular sizes, viz: Small fives, large do., up to eights. Halves, holding one-half gallon, and ones, holding one gallon, with covers to match.

The charcoal crucible is made by lining an ordinary clay or Hessian crucible with a mixture of charcoal and molasses. The charcoal employed should be very fine, and only just enough molasses used to hold it together. The mixture is then packed into the crucible as tightly as possible, dried slowly, and bored out to any extent desirable.

Sometimes water and gum are substituted for molasses.

Fig. 9.

Fig. 9 represents three kinds of charcoal lined crucibles.

Alumina crucibles for some operations are very satisfactory when intense heat is required, but lime will answer as well.

The choice of a crucible depends upon the nature of the substance to be treated in it, the temperature of the fire, and the time it is to remain exposed to the action of heat.

If a charge be basic the crucible should be basic also, and *vice versa.*

To test a crucible for fusibility, heat a piece of the crucible and see if the corners are rounded, or it is fused on the edges.

For corosive action fuse litharge in the crucible. For permeability fill two crucibles with water and note the time required for it to run out; the one which holds the best being preferable.

The action of sudden changes of temperature may be ascertained by heating suddenly, and cooling first in air and afterwards by plunging in cold water.

ROASTING DISHES, (Fig. 10), and SCORIFIERS, (Fig. 11.) Both dishes and scorifiers are made of refractory clay. They should resist the action of litharge and not be too deep. Painting with water and oxide of iron prevents the cutting by strong bases, to some extent.

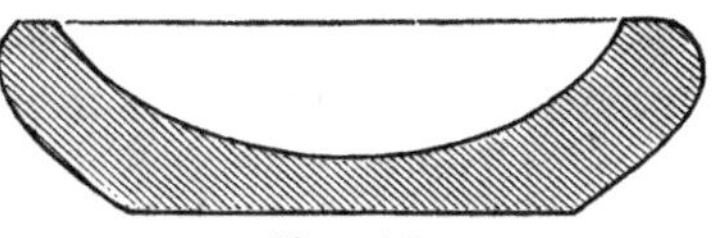

FIG. 10.

FIG. 11.

Scorifiers may be bought or made, but as a rule it is better to buy them as they will stand transportation and require some care to make properly.

A section of a good scorifier is uniform in character. It is close, and should show no flaws or cracks. (Fig. 11*a*.)

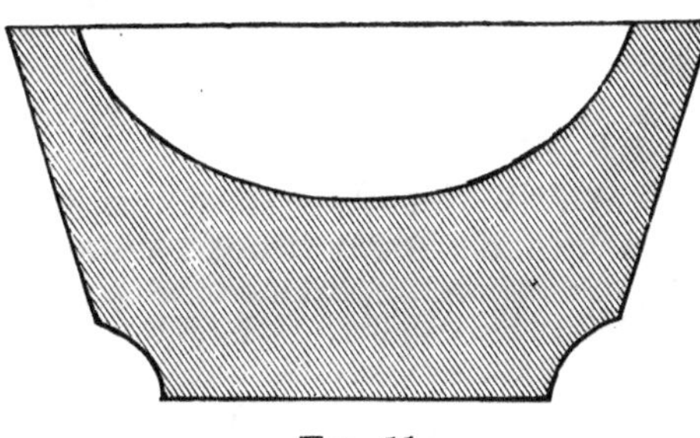

FIG. 11*a*.

CUPELS.

These vessels are generally made of the ashes of burnt bones free from organic matter, ground and washed, horses or sheep bones are said to be the best.

Cupels can be bought or made, but the latter is preferable when they have to be carried some distance. The prepared bone-ash can be obtained in bulk, and is mixed with just sufficient warm water to cause it to hold together without being moist. Sometimes in mixing the bone-ash a little wood ashes is added, or a spoonful of "pearl-ash," (carbonate of potash). Before adding it to the bone-ash it is dissolved in water.

Too much bone-ash should not be mixed at once, as it dries quickly.

If the bone-ash is too fine or too coarse it works badly; as in the first case the cupel will crack upon drying, and in the second, be too porous, absorb silver with the litharge and occasion loss.

The cupel is formed by filling and driving the prepared bone-ash into a mould for the purpose.

The right degree of compression should be used, as otherwise the cupel will be either too hard or too porous. A little experience will tell the operator when he has reached the proper point, when completed it presents the appearance of Fig. 12.

Fig. 12.

Care should be used in drying, plenty of time being allowed, and all moisture and organic matter expelled previous to using, by heating in a furnace. Sometimes a cupel is made of coarse bone-ash, and the surface finished off with fine washed material.

Cupels dried in the sun are better than those dried artificially. They are not so liable to crack.

In the Royal Mint, London, England, a very fine form of cupel is in use. It is square, with four depressions for holding the same number of buttons, enabling the operator to run two assays in duplicate in the same cupel. Iron-bound cupels are sometimes used when the amount to be cupelled is large, especially in treating sweeps.

LUTES, CEMENTS AND WASHES.

Good Fire Lutes.

1. Fire clay, two parts.

Sharp sand, eight parts.

Horse dung, one part.

Mix well and temper the same as mortar, until the desired consistency is reached.

2. Fire clay, one part.

Sand, three parts.

Mix with a little hair and borax water.

3. Zinc cement.

Dissolve three per cent. of borax in water to about 1.49 specific gravity and then add calcined oxide of zinc to suit.

OTHER LUTES.

Plaster of paris mixed with water, milk, glue, or starch water makes a good lute, and will stand a red heat. Wax or parafine is useful for bottles, stoppers, etc., also tallow or stearic acid.

A fine lute for iron vessels is porcelain clay (kaolin) mixed with a solution of borax in water.

A good lute for glass vessels, is quicklime slacked in the air and then beaten into a liquid paste with whites of eggs.

Where corrosive vapors are liable to escape a lute made of fire clay, and boiled linseed oil should be applied and covered with slips of linen spread with the lute of lime and egg.

TO LINE CRUCIBLES.

Fine sifted charcoal mixed with gum water, borax water, or molasses enough to hold when pressed together in the hand, without being wet or sticky. It should contain no lumps.

WASH FOR CRUCIBLES AND SCORIFIERS.

1st. Finely pulverized chalk and water.

2d. Sesquioxide of iron (hematite) and water.

TOOLS.

The tools required by the assayer are regulated more or less by the work to be done.

The following are the principal:

Crucible tongs (Fig. 13.) They should be made with long

Fig. 13.

handles for taking crucibles out of the fire, etc.

Scorification tongs. (Fig. 14.) The spring should not be

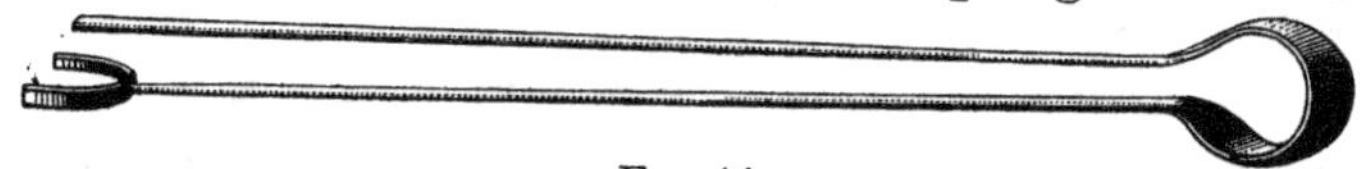

Fig. 14.

too strong, and the horse shoe part should just fit the scorifier.

Cupel tongs. (Fig. 15.) These should be made of steel

Fig. 15.

and about two and one-half feet long with an easy spring.

Three hammers are useful. One large for hammering metal, one medium for breaking crucibles and scorifiers, and one small for marking lead buttons.

A set of small steel dies from 0 to 9 inclusive; and large and small alphabet for marking buttons and bullion will be found useful, but are not necessary.

Three pokers are convenient, small, large, and medium.

One or two small hoes or scrapers for cleaning out the bottom of the cupel muffle. (Fig. 16.)

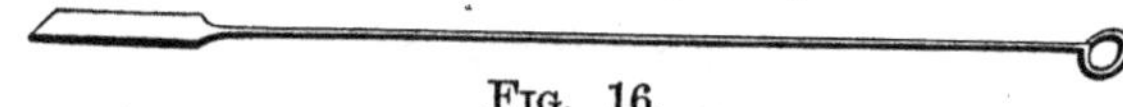

Fig. 16.

A pair of cutting shears and wire snippers for cutting wire for lead assay, etc.

A small vice and anvil, medium size, also a suitable bench for the same.

Wooden mallets, light and heavy, for packing crucibles, making cupels, etc.

Files for sampling and cutting, and several cold chisels. Charcoal saw for blow-pipe charcoal, and crucible tops.

Two iron mortars and pestles, and if much ore is to be pulverized, a grinding plate and rubber, as shown in Fig. 17, will be a great convenience and save labor. The plate is a flat iron casting 18×24 inches, and 1 inch thick. The surface used being planed smooth. The rubber or grinder is a piece of cast iron, 4×6 inches square, 1¼ inches in the middle, by ⅞ of an inch thick at the ends; thus giving a slightly convex surface, which should be true on the board at all points. To conduct the operation place the left hand upon the rubber, throwing the weight of the body upon it, and then grasping the handle with the right hand, move the iron rubber back and forth, depressing the handle when pushing forward and raising it in drawing back.

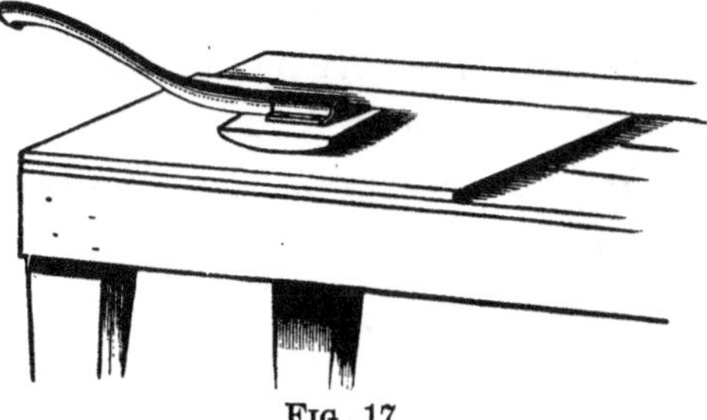
FIG. 17.

The operation is much more rapid than in the ordinary mortar and pestle style, and the manipulator after a little practice has complete control over the ore treated.

Should it not be convenient to have the plate and rubber, a long handled pestle coming up to the chest will be found an improvement, as the mortar can be placed on the floor and the pestle worked while the operator is in a standing position.

A series of sieves, from twenty to one hundred mesh, will be useful for sifting ores and fluxes. The box sieve, (Fig. 18), is a simple arrangement, and consists of a round tin

Fig. 18.

box with a sieve fitting into it as represented in the engraving. The sieve is a tin frame with any desired mesh gauze soldered to it, and fits tightly in the box. The advantage gained by its use is that in sifting the pulverized ore there is no dust. The fine material being passed through the sieve is kept from flying around. The size most convenient is 8 inches in diameter, the box 2 inches deep, and the rim of the sieve 1½ inches, fitting about ¾ inch into the box.

Open and closed ingot moulds for casting lead and silver bars, ingots, etc.

Hand button rolls for gold and silver only. They should be kept covered and free from dust.

Cupel mould, (Fig. 19.). This consists of two parts, an iron ring and a steel pestle or driver, just fitting into the ring.

Fig. 19.

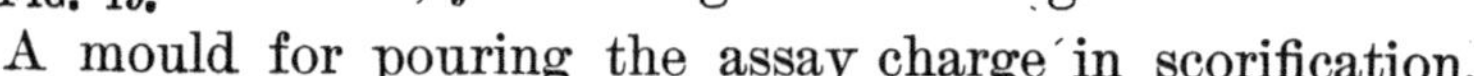

A mould for pouring the assay charge in scorification. (Fig. 20.) This should be of sheet iron or copper, and not too thin. It saves much time, and by employing it, the scorifiers can be used again.

Fig. 20.

Shovels for coke and coal, also a small hatchet for splitting kindling wood. The coke shovel should be ribbed or perforated so that the fine coke or dust may fall through.

Mixing scoops of Russia sheet iron 3½ by 5 inches, with straight sides and back about ¾ inch high. They are convenient for mixing lead or silver crucible charges in, and owing to the high finish of the iron, the assay on being poured out does not cling to the scoop; a few sharp taps detaching everything.

Fig. 21.

A tin sampler, shown in Fig. 21, will be found very useful. It consists of a series of troughs arranged in a row and fastened together at equal distances by a tin strip soldered on their ends. A shovel full of ore emptied by a series of shakes upon them, is just half caught by the troughs; one-half going through the openings between. By repeating this operation, the size of the sample can be reduced to any extent desired.

A laboratory desk, as shown in Figs. 22 and 23, will be

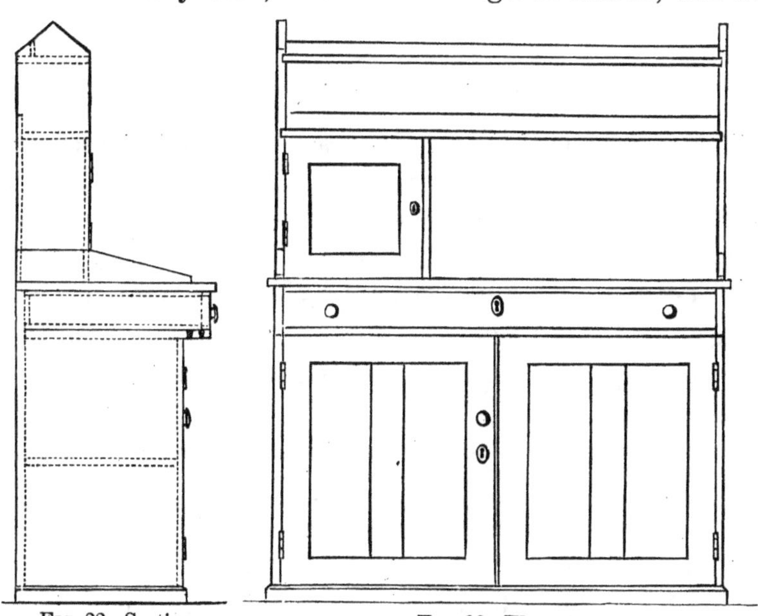

Fig. 22. Section.
Scale ½ inch to the foot.

Fig. 23. Elevation.
Scale ½ inch to the foot.

found a very suitable arrangement, and very compact, consisting of four parts, shelves for bottles, closet for ore-scales, drawer for cupels and apparatus, and double closet for crucibles, scorifiers, etc. The illustrations being made to a scale, the desk can be constructed from them without trouble.

This style of desk has been in use in the School of Mines, New York, for some years, and has been found most convenient. The lower closet should be provided with a shelf and the drawer with partitions. If gas can be had, each desk in a laboratory should have a burner above for lighting purposes, and two or three large jets to which rubber tubes can be fastened so that Bunsen burners can be employed on the desk. These jets are best placed next the scale closet.

APPARATUS.

The amount and kind of apparatus required by the assayer varies ; but the following list will be found about all that will be needed for ordinary work :

About three dozen quart bottles for reagents, glass stoppered. One dozen parting bottles, glass stoppered for bullion assay. Eight oz. is a good size. The stoppers should be square-topped and fit exactly, so that the bottles will not leak when shaken.

An assortment of corked bottles of different sizes for samples.

Two or three ring stands and the same number of Bunsen burners or alcohol lamps. The former are preferable, if gas can be had, and should be provided with two or three feet of rubber tubing for each burner.

Two wash bottles, one small and one large, say one-half pint and pint.

One half-dozen horn spatulas or spoons for mixing ore. Some iron pans for roasting. The ordinary long handled frying pan is suitable, and should be about the size of the furnace top. Before roasting it should be lined with chalk or oxide of iron. One dozen parting flasks, (Fig. 24,) for gold bullion assay; also annealing cups for the same purpose. These are of clay and made thin, (Fig. 25.)

FIG. 24.  FIG. 25.

Brushes for ores and fluxes made of camel's hair; or a large feather trimmed, makes an excellent substitute.

A few dozen sheets of glazed paper, or stout manilla paper when glazed paper cannot be had, for mixing ore upon. Black is preferable, and when held up to the light, there should be no small holes.

Hessian and French crucibles and covers of various sizes and shapes.

Scorifiers, large and small.

Scorification and cupel muffles to suit furnaces.

Cupels from ¾ to 1¼ inches in diameter.

These should always weigh more than the button to be cupelled.

Glass beakers and rods. Funnels for filtering. Gum labels, note book, towels, large and small porcelain mortars, balances, scales and weights, as have been described.

For volumetric work, silver bullion, etc., graduated flasks, pipettes and burettes, will also be necessary. See bullion assay, page 102.

Should the assayer wish to be prepared for all kinds of work, it would be well for him to provide himself with the complete list on pages 167 and 168, appendix, or at least iron, clay and glass retorts, agate mortar (large), one or two platinum crucibles and dishes, and a couple of Bunsen battery cells.

REAGENTS AND CHEMICALS.

These may be divided into six classes.

a. Reducing. To this class belong those bodies which have the power of removing oxygen from its combinations.

b. Oxidizing. All bodies which give up oxygen with facility.

c. Desulphurizing. This class includes all substances which possess a strong affinity for sulphur, and will decompose its compounds under the action of heat or in solution.

d. Sulphurizing. Sulphur and such of its compounds as give up their sulphur easily upon elevation of temperature or in solution.

e. Fluxes. Under this head, we include a large class of bodies, but generally they are substances which render others to which they are added more fusible. Either by acting as a solvent or as a decomposing agent. Fluxes are either acid, basic, or neutral in their action.

f. Solvents include solutions which are used in the wet way only. Such as distilled water, nitric, sulphuric and hydrochloric acids, etc.

g. Precipitants in the wet way. As in the salt solution used in the bullion assay.

The following are the principle reagents and chemicals employed by the assayer in his work. There are, however, many others which might be used, but they can all be classed under the heads just given.

Bicarbonate of Soda (sodic bicarbonate, $NaHCO_3$) or the corresponding potash salt. These act as desulphurising agents, and in some cases as oxidising agents.

The latter action being due to the carbonic acid contained. Sometimes they act as basic fluxes.

They should be free from moisture, and lumps. On account of their easy fusibility they can retain in suspension, without losing their fluidity, a large proportion of finely powdered infusible substances.

LITHARGE (PbO), is a basic flux, oxydizing and desulphurizing agent, and supplies the lead in the gold and silver crucible assay. It should be dry, and free from red oxide of lead, as the latter has the power of oxydizing silver, and thus causing loss of that metal during the assay. To free litharge from the red oxide, fuse the same in a crucible, and pour the mass into a cold ingot-mould, keeping it from the air while cooling. All litharge before using should be well sampled, and assayed for silver. To do this, charge in a crucible—

Litharge............	4 A.T.
Soda...............	2 "
Charcoal	1 gm.

and cover with a layer of dried salt, one-quarter of an inch thick. Fuse in a hot fire until completely liquid, then withdraw, and proceed as in the assay of a silver ore (p. 66). White lead (carbonate of lead—plumbic carbonate $PbCO_3$), is sometimes employed instead of litharge; also, acetate of lead for delicate experiments.

BORAX, CRYSTALLIZED ($2NaBO_2.B_2O_3+10H_2O$).—This acts as an acid flux; but, on account of the water contained, it is generally employed in a vitrified condition, or borax glass ($2NaBO_2.B_2O_3$), which has a more intensified effect. It has neither an oxydizing or desulphurizing action.

To prepare—Fuse the commercial borax in a chalk-lined crucible, pouring the fused mass out on a clean surface to cool. Pulverize, and keep in a glass-stoppered bottle. As borax, when heated, loses its water of crystallization, and undergoes an immense increase in volume, only a little should be added at a time in fusing. Boracic acid (H_3BO_3) is also sometimes used.

SILICA (SiO_2), acts as a good acid flux, and can often be used with advantage. A good substitute is glass ($Na_2Si_3O_7+CaSi_3O_7+SiO_2$), as it is easily fusible, and forms a good slag. It should be powdered and free from moisture. Lime glass is the best.

BLACK FLUX, SUBSTITUTE.—A mixture of three parts flour and ten parts of bi-carbonate of soda acts as a flux and reducing agent, and is especially useful in the lead assay. Black Flux, proper=1 of nitre and 3 of argol—deflagrated.

CYANIDE OF POTASSIUM (potassic cyanide KCy=KCN), as a flux for reducing and desulphurizing is invaluable. It should be prepared with care and kept in a tight bottle, as it absorbs moisture. Take the ordinary commercial article and pulverize in an iron mortar as fine as possible. Never sift, as the dust is *poisonous*. To protect yourself, cover the mortar with a towel, or a board having a hole in the centre for the pestle.

FERRO-CYANIDE OF POTASSIUM (yellow prussiate of potash)(potassic ferro-cyanide $K_4Cfy=4KCY,FeCy_2$), will often be found useful as a flux for reducing and desulphurizing. The crystallized material should be powdered in a porcelain mortar, and dried over a slow fire until it is almost white. If the heat is too high it will carbonize and turn brown.

ARGOL ($KHC_4H_4O_6$), crude bitartrate of potash, acts as a basic flux and reducing agent. It should be pulverized and dry, and its reducing power determined. For this purpose we charge

Argol................	2 gms
Litharge............	2 A.T.
Soda................	½ "

in a crucible, fuse in a hot fire, cool, extract the button and weigh in grammes. Dividing by two gives the amount of lead one gramme of argol will reduce from litharge.

CHARCOAL, acts as a reducing agent and desulphurizer. It should be finely powdered and its reducing power determined, as in the case of argol. Using one gramme instead of two as in that assay. Ordinary wood charcoal will reduce twenty-eight grammes of lead from litharge.

STARCH n($C_6H_{10}O_5$)($C_{12}H_{22}O_{11}$), sugar, and gum, may also be used for reducing agents, but are not so convenient.

Dried starch reduces thirteen parts of lead. Common starch about eleven and one-half parts. Sugar fourteen and one-half, and gum arabic eleven parts. For some purposes pure hydrogen gas will be found essential as in the assay of oxide of tin. It is the strongest and best reducing agent, but requires care in its preparation. It is made by dissolving zinc in dilute sulphuric acid, and passing the gas evolved through oil of vitrol, to dry it before using. One part of hydrogen will reduce about one hundred and four parts of lead from litharge.

METALLIC IRON (Fe), is a desulphurizing agent, and is indispensable, especially in the assay of lead ores. The best form is iron wire about ⅛ inch in diameter. Nails and filings may also be used.

PURE LEAD (Pb), in sheet or granulated form, is used principally in the assay of silver ores. It acts as a basic flux, and a solvent or wash for the precious metals. The sheet form is useful in cupelling gold and silver beads, and in the bullion assay. The granulated is essential in the scorification assay.

It can be obtained pure by decomposing the best white lead by charcoal, and granulating or fusing in bars, as the case may require.

In sections where granulated lead free from silver, or white lead, cannot be obtained, the assayer can make his own granulated lead from bar lead, poor in silver, by the following method:—Melt about fifty pounds of bar lead in an iron pot or crucible, and keep it just at the melting point. Then pour a ladleful of the melted lead into a wooden bread-tray which has been well chalked on the inside. Keep this agitated by gently rocking the tray to prevent solidification, and when the mass begins to get pasty, throw it into the air and catch it again repeatedly until cold, when the metal will be found to be nearly all granulated. Sift through a twenty-mesh sieve, and what does not go through re-melt. The whole fifty pounds can be granulated in this way in two hours. After granulation sample well and test about thirty to fifty grammes for silver, by the scorification assay. In using the lead, the silver contained in it must be deducted from the results in assaying an ore.

NITRE (potassic nitrate KNO_3), acts as a basic flux and oxydizing agent. It should be finely powdered, dry, and assayed for its oxydizing power. Charge:

Nitre	3 gms.
Charcoal	1 "
Litharge	2 A.T.
Soda	1 "

Place in a Hessian crucible and cover with salt. Fuse in a hot fire, remove, cool and weigh. The difference between the weight of the button obtained and that given in the assay of charcoal, divided by three, gives the oxydizing power of nitre per gramme.

Powdered Lime (CaO), (dry), and fluor spar ($Ca F_2$), will often be found useful as basic fluxes, especially in the assay of iron ores. Magnesia (Mgo), and alúmina (Al_2O_3) or kaolin ($Al_2 O_3.2SiO_2$)—are also used, and cryolite ($3NaF.AlF_3$) for tin ores.

As Sulphurizing Agents: powdered sulphur (S), pure galena (PbS), or sulphide of antimony (Sb_2S_3), are employed.

Carbonate of Ammonia (ammonic carbonate $(NH_4)_2CO_3$), as a desulphurizing agent, is used in the decomposition of some sulphates, as sulphate of copper, in roasting. It should be powdered and kept in a close vessel.

Common Salt (sodic chloride NaCl), as a cover and wash, and as a reagent in the bullion assay, should be always kept on hand. The purer it is the better, and it must also be fine and dry.

As Solvents and Precipitants—distilled water (H_2O), sulphuric acid (H_2SO_4), nitric acid (HNO_3), hydrochloric acid (HCl), chloride of sodium, nitrate of silver (argentic nitrate $AgNO_3$), and sulphuretted hydrogen (H_2S), are most frequently employed.

The acids may be purchased pure. Nitric acid should be free from chlorine, which can be separated by the addition of nitrate of silver, drop by drop, until a precipitate ceases to form. The clear acid, after settling, being drawn off with a syphon.

Nitrate of silver may be made by dissolving pure silver in nitric acid free from chlorine; evaporate to dryness and dissolve one part of the salt in twenty parts of distilled water.

Sulphuretted hydrogen is best prepared from powdered sulphide of iron (ferrous sulphide FeS) and dilute sulphuric acid. The gas being passed through a second bottle filled with water to wash it. Fig. 26 shows the apparatus in position for use The glass tubes are connected with small pieces of rubber tubing. The gas may be passed into a solution to be precipitated, or a water solution may be saturated and used at pleasure. The sulphide of iron can be made by heating scrap iron or borings to a red heat in a crucible and throwing in sulphur. The sulphide produced may be then fused or broken up, still-fusion is unnecessary.

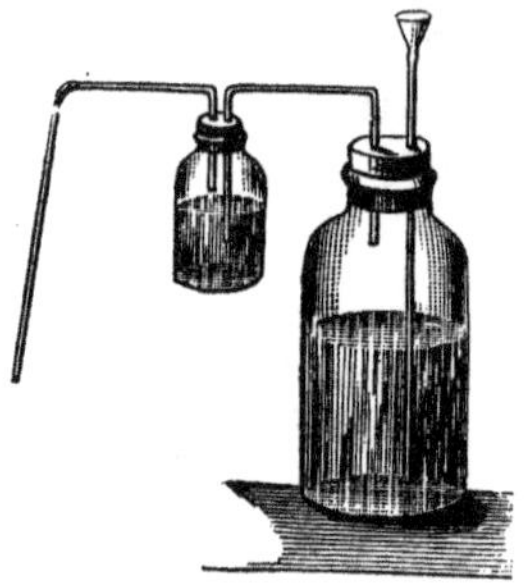

FIG. 26.

OTHER CHEMICALS and reagents will often be found necessary if assays in the wet way are to be made, but the reader must be referred to page 168. The most important are arsenic (As), arsenide of iron (ferrous arsenide Fe_2As), hyposulphite ($Na_2H_2S_2O_4$) and sulphide of sodium (Na_2S).

PRELIMINARY TESTING OF ORES.

Before breaking up a sample it should be thoroughly examined to determine, if possible, its mineralogical character, and if this is impossible it should be tested with the blowpipe, by the scheme and table pp. 157-164, appendix.

By the result of the blowpipe assay the assayer can settle upon what method he will pursue, and often save much time. The determination of the presence of gold will decide the question of crucible or scorification assay. Arsenic antimony or sulphur, that of roasting, etc. With a little practice the assayer will seldom have to use the blowpipe when the specimen is in lump. The color, hardness, weight and general appearance indicating the nature of the ore, and consequently the method of assay; all powdered samples must, of course, be tested by the blowpipe.

SAMPLING AND PULVERIZING.

The selection and preparation of the sample for assay may be called the "secret of success." It is the most important operation which the assayer has to conduct; and unless the sample be well taken his work will be useless.

No matter how large or how small the amount of ore he may be called upon to treat, the same care is necessary in the sampling; for one portion may be very rich and another portion valueless, so far as the metal sought for is concerned. The sample, therefore, taken for an assay, must *always* be an *average* of all the ore.

The method of sampling an ore depends upon its constitution:

a.—The ore contains no metallic particles.

b.—The ore contains metallic particles.

In the first case the operation is comparatively easy. If there is a large quantity of ore to be sampled, it is broken up more or less finely; the degree of fineness depending upon the amount of ore from which the lot for assay is to be taken; and is then either thrown upon a sampler, page 33, or divided by piling it in a heap and cutting it in quarters, one of which may be selected to be again broken up and quartered, and so on until a sample sufficiently small for assay is obtained; or an equal portion of each quarter may be taken, and the four portions well mixed, broken up, thrown in a heap, and the operation repeated until the required sample is reached. If there is only a single specimen or lot obtained by a sampling as above, it is better to crush it, and pass it all through a sixty or eighty-mesh sieve; the finer the better. The pulverized ore is then well mixed with a spoon or spatula on glazed paper, and the amount for assay weighed out by taking a little here and there, or dividing into quarters and taking some from each.

The fine ore should never be shaken to mix it, or poured upon the scale pan directly from the vessel in which it is contained.

b.—The ore contains metallic particles.

The sample may be selected from the heap of ore in the same manner as described under *a*, but a larger lot must be taken for assay and the whole pulverized and passed through an eighty-mesh sieve, which will divide the ore into two portions:

1st. Siftings.

2d. Metallic residue.

The siftings must be well mixed and sampled upon glazed paper, as above.

The metallic residue must be tested as a whole and *not* sampled.

The method of making the assay and calculation of results will be given hereafter.

Care must be taken in preparing a sample that all apparatus employed is clean, especially the mortars and sieves. The first can be cleaned by pulverizing a little sand in them, or using a pumice-stone pestle, and the latter by rubbing with a clean towel or rapping upon a bench.

The box sieve, (page 28), will be found very convenient,

and better than the ordinary kind, as it prevents the loss of dust which would alter the value of the sample more or less. The sieve should be used for nothing but ores, and carefully cleaned after each operation.

To sample bullion, chip from alternate corners above and below; or else melt and take the first and last pouring. To sample coin: for silver, stamp out small pieces from the center and edge. Gold coins, cut slips running from the center to the circumference.

WEIGHING ORE AND REAGENTS.

The ore, litharge, test lead, oxydizing and reducing agents, should be weighed accurately.

The ordinary fluxes may be weighed approximately, still, it is better to weigh close, as more uniform results are obtained.

The same pans of either the flux or ore balance should always be used for the weights, and the latter must be handled with the pincers provided for that purpose. The ore scales should be kept free from dust, and be adjusted before each weighing, for next to the sampling the weighing of the ore is most important.

When a number of charges of the same ore are to be weighed, weigh out the fluxes first, and then add the ore in order. In this way the work will be greatly facilitated.

Instead of weighing the test lead and pure lead, they can be measured. A very simple and good test lead measure is a glass tube about ¼ of an inch in diameter, in which a cork is fitted to slide up and down. The tube being graduated for known weights. As far as possible glazed paper or watch glasses should be used in weighing, to prevent substances from touching the scale pan, especially in employing the quantitative analytical balance.

If the substance is one which is liable to absorb moisture from the air it should be weighed between watch glasses, fastened with a clip. Cyanides must never be weighed upon the pan direct.

The balance pans of the bullion and quantitative balance should never be handled with the fingers or set upon a rough surface.

CALCINATION AND ROASTING.

In calcination the object is to drive off moisture, while in roasting the operation is conducted in such a manner as to ensure oxidation, and the elimination of sulphur, arsenic, antimony, etc. To calcine a substance it is not necessary that the air should have free access, or that the material treated be stirred.

A high temperature is seldom necessary, 212°–220° F. being sufficient.

Crucibles will be found the most convenient vessels for calcining.

For roasting, combustion must take place, and consequently the vessels employed, must be open and flat to allow the oxygen of the air to act freely. The ore must be stirred continually, and when easily fusible, be mixed with some substance to prevent agglutination. Charcoal, graphite, or sand may be used for this purpose. The heat should be low at first, and raised toward the end of the operation, and in some cases chemicals mixed with the mass hasten the process, and render it more complete; as in the addition of carbonate of ammonia in roasting copper ores. The operation may be performed on a crucible furnace in an iron pan lined with chalk or oxide of iron ; or in an open vessel like a scorifier, (Fig. 10), in a muffle furnace. In any case the draft of air should be strong, as the fumes are injurious.

A very nice stirrer for this operation can be made from a piece of ordinary wire, by doubling it, and bending down the loop like a small hoe ; the ends of the wire being twisted together to form a handle.

REDUCTION AND FUSION.

Reduction is simply the removal of the oxygen from the body acted upon ; generally by the action of substances having a stronger affinity for it.

The operation of reduction is usually accompanied by fusion, which is simply melting, although they may act independently of each other. Reduction and fusion are carried on in crucibles and scorifiers, etc.

The heat required is higher than that necessary for the foregoing operations, consequently the draft should be stronger, and for this reason wind furnaces are employed. Fusion is sometimes a preliminary step to oxidation and sublimation.

To perform the operation of reduction in a muffle furnace, the muffle must be partially filled with charcoal, and the mouth closed.

DISTILLATION AND SUBLIMATION.

Distillation may be divided into two cases :

a.—When a solid is acted upon.

b.—When a liquid is acted upon.

The product is generally liquid.

Sublimation is similar to distillation, but the product is solid.

Both operations may be conducted in flasks, retorts, or crucibles; but usually in the operation of distillation a cooled condenser is necessary, as in the process of making distilled water. The term "destructive distillation" is used where the body acted upon undergoes decomposition.

SCORIFICATION AND CUPELLATION.

Scorification and cupellation may be called a combination of fusion, roasting and sublimation, the difference being, that in the latter case the volatile compounds formed are absorbed by the cupel, while in the former they form a slag. Both will be described in detail hereafter. (See assay of silver ores.)

INQUARTATION AND PARTING.

Under this head comes the separation of alloys, and the treatment of the buttons from the gold and silver assay.

Inquartation is the process of alloying gold with silver to form a more soluble alloy, while parting is the separation of metals by solution, and includes the same.

WEIGHING BEADS AND BULLION.

This operation must be conducted with the greatest care, and the balance adjusted both before and after weighing. Before weighing, the bead or bullion should be well cleaned with a small brush. To weigh the buttons of the base metals the ore scales are sufficiently accurate; but for weighing silver and gold, the bullion balance must be employed. The weights should be counted on the pan, and the spaces in the box as a check.

It is best to keep the bullion balance in a separate room from the laboratory, where it will be free from dust and fumes. It should also stand upon a firm shelf, to prevent shaking. In determining a weight, do not use the weights at random, but find the nearest single weight, and add the others in regular order, until the required combination is reached.

In duplicate assays the buttons should balance each other, or very nearly so.

To facilitate the weighing out of pure silver in the bullion assay, Mr. W. S. Ward of the U. S. Assay Office, in the city of New York, has devised a series of standard disks, which run from fifty to five hundred milligrammes, and by combining one or more almost any desired weight can be obtained, thus saving labor and time. When obtaining a weight the door of the balance should be kept closed, and the number of divisions marked by the needle observed, and on which side of the centre-line they are. Each division counts 1-10 of a milligramme on the second swing, and the total can be either added or deducted from the weights in the pan, as the case may be; if the button is heaviest, add, if lightest, subtract. On the quantitative balance the rider indicates milligrammes and fractions of the same. So that in obtaining the final weight after the pans are nearly balanced, the door can be closed and the rider adjusted by means of the rod from the right-hand side. Never lean on the balance shelf in weighing or leave the rider on. The first may throw the balance out of adjustment. The second, cause error in the next weighing.

TABULATING RESULTS.

Reporting.—In making an assay each result should be noted as obtained, and nothing left to memory. Care should also be observed in arranging and reporting. To facilitate this, a series of blanks will be found on pages 142–149, from which a choice can be made.

The report should be made as simple and comprehensive as possible, and written in terms which a business man can understand.

It should also indicate in the case of gold and silver the ounces Troy to the ton avoirdupois, and the value, in gold, per ton, of ore. Gold being taken at $20.67 per oz. Troy. Silver variable. The value by the old U. S. standard being $1.29 per oz.

Base metals are reported in percentage. Bullion, the number of parts in a thousand, or fineness.

PART II.

FIRE ASSAYS.

LEAD. *Symbol*—Pb.

SOURCES.—The principal ores of lead are:

Galena (sulphide) (PbS), ... Pure=86.6 lead
Cerrusite (carbonate) ($PbCO_3$), ... " =77.52 "
Anglesite (sulphate) ($PbSO_4$), ... " =68.31 "
Pyromorphite (phosphate and chloride)
($3Pb3P_2O_5+PbCl_2$), ... " =68.59 "

But lead also enters into the composition of many minerals although seldom in workable quantities.

ASSAY.—The assay of lead may be performed either in the crucible or muffle furnace. The methods of treating varying with the ores. The object of the assayer being in all cases to decompose the ore treated, and obtain a button of lead.

Methods applicable to sulphides, etc.:

1ST.	2D.	3D.
Ore.............10 gms.	Ore............10 gms.	Ore............10 gms.
Black Flux Substitute } ...25 "	Soda, Bi-Carb...20 "	Ferro Cyanide of Potassium....20 "
3 Loops Iron Wire, Points down.	3 Iron Nails Points down.	Cyanide of Potassium.........10 "
Salt..............Cover.	Salt.............Cover.	Salt..............Cover.

The charges should be well mixed, placed in a crucible, and covered with salt. The wires or iron nails being added in such a manner that they can be drawn out quickly after fusion.

The crucible must be covered while in the fire and during the process of cooling.

In the first and second methods a double sulphide of soda

and lead is formed, which is acted upon by the iron present. The carbon acting also as a reducing and desulphurizing agent.

4TH.

Ore................	10	gms.
Soda Bi. Carb.....	20	"
Argol.............	5	"
Flour.............	2	"
Borax (unfused)...	1	"

The ore and first three fluxes are mixed and placed in a small Hessian crucible, which will go into the muffle of the cupel furnace. The borax is then added, and three nails or two pieces of iron wire bent into the form of hairpins stuck into the mass ; after which a cover of salt ¼-inch thick, is packed upon the whole charge.

Several assays can be run in a muffle at once, but care in heating should be observed. The muffle should be at a bright cherry-red when the assays are introduced, and the heat raised until the salt cover fuses. This will take about twenty minutes, after which the muffle is made white hot for about ten minutes, when a perfectly fluid fusion is obtained. The assays are then withdrawn, the wires carefully taken out, the crucibles tapped gently, and the contents poured into a mould. This operation must be performed carefully and quickly, to prevent solidification of the slag. The iron and carbonaceous material act as already explained.

5TH.

Ore...............	10	gms.
Cyanide of Potassium	20 to 25	"
Salt..............		cover

Fuse in a moderate fire twelve to fifteen minutes, keeping the crucible covered while in the fire and cooling.

The cyanide of potassium takes the sulphur from the lead forming a sulpho-cyanide of potassium.

Methods applicable to oxidized ores and carbonates:

1st.

Ore...............	10 gms.
Argol	5 "
Soda Bi-Carb......	20 "
Salt...............	cove.

Mix well and heat slowly for about twelve minutes, and then strongly until in complete fusion. Remove from the fire, cool and break.

The argol in this case acts as the reducing agent, owing to its carbon.

For treatment of cupel bottoms add ten grammes borax glass.

2d.

Ore................	10 gms.
Black flux, sub.....	35 "
Salt.................	cover.

Fuse in a hot fire, and in some cases where the material treated contains substances fusible with difficulty, borax glass may be added to facilitate the fusion.

The lead assay is not accurate for several reasons, chiefly because of the volatility of the lead, and the presence of substances which alloy with the button.

Antimony and zinc in an ore interferes with the assay; as the first will generally be found with the lead, while the zinc, though driven off, carries lead with it.

When much antimony is present, the following method may be advantageously employed. (Mitchell, pages 379–380).

Ore...............	10 gms.
Carb. of potash....	35 "
Saltpetre..........	1 "
Salt...............	cover.

The assay is performed in a muffle furnace, and requires about thirty minutes for fusion, then ten minutes slow cooling, which is done by opening the door of the muffle, and decreasing the heat. Finally finishing with closed muffle, and a high heat for ten minutes, when the crucibles are removed, cooled and broken. Most of the antimony remains in the slag. This method requires care and practice. Very often in making an assay in the muffle the crucibles, being small at the bottom, fall over. To avoid this, make a little platform of clay for each crucible.

REMARKS.—Pure galena, treated by the foregoing methods, for sulphides, gave the following :

METHODS.	RESULTS.
No. 1	78.4 and 78.6
" 2	73. " 73.4
" 3	78.5 " 79.1

The assay by cyanide gives lower results, but cleaner buttons.

The yield by muffle assay is good, duplicates agreeing within 2 per cent.

The first method for carbonates gives weights varying from 1 to 2 per cent.

Care is required in fireing.

ANTIMONY. *Symbol*—Sb.

SOURCES. — The principal ore of antimony is the sulphide—called stibnite, or grey antimony ore ($Sb_2 S_3$)—which contains, when pure, 71.98 per cent. of metal. Antimony is also found native alloyed with other metals, and in combination with oxygen.

ASSAY.—In the assay of antimony ore, the assayer may be required to determine one of two things.

a. The pure sulphide of antimony (antimonium crudum), which the ore may contain.

b. The metallic antimony (regulus of antimony), which the ore may yield.

a. Determination of the sulphide. As sulphide of antimony fuses at a low red heat, it is not changed in its character if the air is excluded, so that the following method may be adopted:

Charge the broken ore into a crucible the bottom of which is perforated, and just fits into a second crucible about half its depth. Then cover and lute the lid and the joint between the two crucibles with fire clay and sand. The upper crucible only should be heated, and to effect this the lower can extend into the ash-pit of the furnace, being supported by an inverted crucible or a brick.

The sulphide of antimony will melt and collect in the under crucible, while the silicious and earthy matter remains in the upper.

b. Determination of metallic antimony. 1st. The ore is oxidized.

Ore...............	10 gms.
Black flux sub.....	25 "
Argol.............	1 "
Salt..............	cover.

This assay is conducted in the same manner as the lead assay, only the heat must be regulated with more care, and the assay taken from the fire as soon as finished. The cover being left on.

The flour in the black flux substitute, and the argol, act as the reducing agents, metallic antimony being produced.

2d. The ore is a sulphide.

Ore...............10 gms.
Cyanide of potassium,
35–40 "
Salt............... cover.

The charge should be well mixed, the heat low, and the operation performed quickly; observing the same precautions in cooling as before.

REMARKS.—The result obtained in assaying for antimony cannot be accepted as the correct amount of metal in the ore; it only represents the possible yield, and the button often contains other metals besides, which have been reduced with the antimony in the ore, when the latter is not pure. It should, therefore, be tested for iron, etc., alloyed with the antimony. The button should be cleaned by washing, not hammered, to detach the slag, as it is brittle.

When much iron and siliceous matter is contained in the ore, the method for the determination of the sulphide does not give good results. Two assays of impure stibnite gave 44.5 and 44.2 per cent.

To separate from foreign metals, break the button and dissolve in concentrated nitric acid, which converts the antimony into antimonic acid, which is insoluble. Filter, wash, dry and ignite in a porcelain crucible; the weight found multiplied by .7922 equals the metallic antimony. Practically it is not necessary to treat the buttons from the fire assay unless they are very impure.

For some impure ores a very large charge of cyanide (say 50–60 gms.), and a quick, hot fire will be found to give good results.

GOLD AND SILVER. *Symbols*—Au. and Ag.

SOURCES.—All substances containing gold and silver may, for the purposes of the assayer, be divided into two classes:

Class 1st. Minerals or ores, including incidental industrial products.

Class 2d. Metallic gold and silver, and alloys, native or artificial.

Native gold alone occurs in nature sufficiently abundant to acquire any great commercial value. It is found commonly in a quartzose gangue, and nearly always associated with one of the following minerals: Iron and copper pyrites, mispickel or arsenical pyrites, blende, and galena. There are also compounds with tellurium, and native alloys. (See page 134).

The principal sources of silver are silver glance, stephanite, pyrargyrite, kerargyrite, native silver, galena and agentiferous copper ores. But as many minerals contain silver in greater or less quantity, for the convenience of the assayer, a complete list has been arranged on page 133.

The assay of gold and silver comprises.

a. Assay of ores.

b. Assay of alloys, according as we have material of 1 or 2.

a. ASSAY OF ORES.—Assays of gold and silver ores are made in almost the same manner, so that a general description will answer for both. They embrace the following steps:

1st. Preparation of the sample. 2d. Collection of the gold and silver in a lead button. 3d. Cupellation of the lead button. 4th. Weighing the bead. 5th. Inquartation, parting, and cupelling of the gold residue. 6th. Weighing the gold.

Extra care must be observed in sampling gold and silver ores.

2d. The collection of gold and silver in a button of lead is effected in a crucible or scorifier, whence two methods of assay: (*a*). Crucible assay. (*b*). Scorification assay.

The former is applicable to all ores. The latter is limited by the small size of scorifiers, to rich ores. It is not safe to use this method for gold ores, as a very slight error may make a great difference in the results, because of the small quantity of ore necessarily employed.

(*a*.) CRUCIBLE ASSAY.—An ore of gold or silver is composed of precious metals, gangue, oxides, sulphides, etc. To collect the precious metals the ore is mixed with litharge, suitable fluxes, and oxidising or reducing agents, and fused in a crucible. The litharge is reduced to metallic lead, seizes upon the precious metals, and collects at the bottom of the crucible, while the foreign materials form, with the fluxes, a fusible slag above. The crucible is broken when cold, and the button detached from the slag by hammering on an anvil.

The charge: The weight of ore taken depends upon the supposed richness or poverty, since it is required to obtain finally a bead of precious metal for weighing. As a rule it is usual to take one-third assay ton for silver ores, and one, two, or four assay tons for gold ores. All ores require the following reagents: Argol or charcoal, an oxidizing agent (nitre), with invariably a cover of salt. Borax, silica, and other reagents are useful at times, but their employment must be left to the judgment of the assayer, guided by the properties of the reagents, and the composition of the ore. It is well to bear in mind that for basic impurities, an acid flux is used, and for an acid gangue, a basic flux. Unless the charge of ore be very large, as a rule, employ a weight of litharge twice, and carbonate of soda the same as that of the ore. These proportions may be modified according to the composition of the ore. The amount of nitre depends upon the reducing power of the ore. It is added to control the size of the button.

Size of the lead button: There are two limits to the size of the button. (1st.) It must be large enough, or sufficient litharge must be reduced throughout the mass to collect all the precious metals. (2d.) There should not be an excess of lead, which would occasion a loss of silver upon cupellation. A button of fifteen or twenty grammes is the best size for a weight of ore from one-third to four assay tons, and is a good size for cupellation. A button too large for cupellation can be made smaller by scorifying. The reducing power of an ore is due to the presence of sulphur, arsenic, antimony, zinc, etc.

Preliminary Assay of Ores.—Warm the crucible before placing it in the fire, which should be bright, and effect the fusion in the shortest possible time. When the the contents of the crucible are in quiet fusion, withdraw, tap, cool and break. The charge of ore is as follows:

Ore...............	2 gms.
Litharge..........	25 "
Soda Bi-Carb......	10 "
Salt..............	cover.

Three cases may arise here. Two grammes may yield:

1st. No lead, or less than three grammes.

2d. Three grammes of lead.

3d. More than three grammes

Let us suppose we take for assay $\frac{1}{3}$ A. T. of silver ore, and the reducing power of two grammes of ore is 1.5 gms. lead. $\frac{1}{3}$ A. T., or ten grammes of ore, (about), will reduce 7.5 of lead, and as the required button is fifteen grammes, we must add enough argol or charcoal to reduce 7.5 gms. in addition; taking argol as 8.5, we shall require $7.5 \div 8.5 = 0.882$, say one gramme, or charcoal $7.5 \div 28 = 0.268$ say $\frac{1}{3}$ of a gramme.

If the reducing power correspond to the third case, a similar calculation will show how much nitre is needed. In the second case ten grammes of ore would reduce a button of fifteen. The character of the slag obtained in the preliminary assay may suggest some modification of the regular charge. If it be earthy, for instance, we would add borax, glass, or silica. Experience will often enable the assayer to judge of the reducing power without extra assay, by noting the approximate amount of sulphides contained in the ore before pulverizing the same.

ROASTING.—Ores containing a large amount of arsenic, antimony, or zinc, should be roasted. In the former case, if the ore is not roasted there will be danger of the formation of oxysulphurets, which, though fusible, are not decomposed at a white heat, and enter the slag, carrying silver with them. A large quantity of nitre is liable to boil over; even should this not occur, the evolution of vapors puffs up the mass, and lead may be left adhering to the sides of the crucible. Arsenic and antimony produce arseniates and antimoniates, which carry silver into the slag. Zinc also increases the loss of silver by volatilization, and by the slag.

The ore may be roasted conveniently in a cast-iron pan,

over the furnace. The pan should be coated with red ochre, or chalk, which prevents injury to the same, and loss of ore.

The weighed sample must be spread over the pan, and stirred until all danger of fusion is past. The ore must be heated gradually, not above a dull red for some time, and finally to a full red or higher heat. Too high a temperature at the outset causes the fusion of sulphides and the formation of matter troublesome to roast. A rapid disengagement of arsenic, antimony, or zinc will also cause a mechanical loss of silver. Should fusion occur, it is better to weigh out a fresh portion of ore and roast it again. The operation may be considered finished when, after keeping the pan at a dull red heat for some time no fumes can be perceived.

If copper pyrites be present, it is best to mix some carbonate of ammonia with the ore. After the fumes have ceased the pan should be covered ; the sulphates being converted into volatile sulphate of ammonia, which passes off.

Arsenic and antimony require the addition of fine charcoal to reduce arseniates and antimoniates formed in roasting. Care being taken to burn out all the charcoal. If the ore contains a fusible sulphide, as antimony glance or galena, mix with some fine sand before roasting. Ores may be roasted in the muffle, in the earthen saucer already mentioned.

FUSION.—The prepared charge is thoroughly mixed and placed in a crucible. A hot fire is employed, and the crucible removed when complete fusion has taken place. This requires from twenty to twenty-five minutes. The crucible is tapped and when cold broken.

(*b*). SCORIFICATION ASSAY.—The reagents for scorification assay are granulated (pure) lead, and borax glass.

The ore is mixed with these, the mixture put in a scorifier, and fused in a muffle.

An alloy of lead with the precious metals, and a slag composed of litharge with the impurities and gangue of the ore is formed. The proportions of lead and borax will vary and should be greater as the gangue and metallic oxides are more difficult of fusion. The following table shows the proportions found by experience to be adapted to the different gangues. They are referred to one part of ore:

Character of Gangue.	Parts Test Lead.	Parts Borax Glass.
Quartzose	8.	
Basic	8.	0.25—1.00
Galena	5.6	0.15
Arsenical	16.	0.10—0.50
Antimonial	16.	0.10—1.00
Farlerz	12-16	0.10—0.15
Iron pyrites	10-15	0.10—0.20
Blende	10-15	0.10—0.20

In most cases one-tenth of an assay ton of ore and thirty grammes of lead will be found to work well. The ore and one-half the lead are mixed in the bottom of the scorifier, and the rest of the lead poured over the mixture so as to form a cover. Two or three lumps of borax about the size of peas being placed on top. The charge of ore varies from one-third to one-twentieth of an assay ton according to its richness, and if one scorifier will not contain it, weigh equal fractional parts for the number required, rather than to weigh the whole charge and roughly divide it between the scorifiers.

Three distinct periods may be noted in the working of an assay. (1.) Roasting. (2.) Fusion. (3.) Scorification.

A strong heat is maintained at first to melt the lead. This is effected by closing the muffle and increasing the draft. As soon as the lead is fused the muffle is opened, and the ore is seen floating upon the surface of the lead. In a large muffle it is sufficient to place the scorifier in the back part first, and move it forward when the lead is fused.

(1). The roasting commences and is continued at a moderate heat until no more fumes are seen, and the ore has disappeared.

(2). The heat is raised in order to fuse all the material. When the fusion is complete, clear white fumes of lead arise from the scorifier, there is a play of colors across the surface of the lead, and the slag encircles the metallic bath like a ring. The borax glass plays an important part just here, by giving liquidity to the slag, so that it can be thrown to the side as fast as formed, exposing the lead for oxidation. If borax glass is not added and the ore contains a gangue fusible with difficulty, the scoriæ will float in masses over the lead, impeding the oxidation.

(3). When fusion is complete the heat is lowered to a constant point, until the ring of slag, which is continually growing smaller, closes over the lead. Then the heat should again be raised to liquify the slag, and allow the lead to settle, after which the scorifier is removed from the furnace, cooled or poured. Hammer the button as usual. The whole assay occupies from thirty-five to fifty minutes. Too much borax should not be added at first.

It is better to mix only a portion with the ore, and to introduce the rest as needed during the operation.

Galena—Special Method.—It is best to make a scorification assay of galena. If, however, it is desirable to make a crucible assay, a charge of nitre and carbonate of soda is employed, instead of roasting the ore. Twenty grammes of nitre per assay ton are required for pure galena, this amount diminishing as the gangue increases in quantity, or the sulphur is lessened. Employ the same weight of carbonate of soda as of ore. Make a preliminary assay with an assumed charge, and modify the regular charge according to the result.

THE LEAD BUTTON.—The lead button for cupellation must be malleable and of the proper size.

A good cupel will absorb its own weight of litharge, but it is better to use a cupel one-third as heavy again as the button. The cupels in ordinary use weigh about eighteen grammes. If a button be too large it may be reduced in size by scorification; there is less loss in this operation than in cupellation. A brittle button may be due to arsenic, antimony, zinc, or litharge, and must be scorified before cupellation, with lead, if necessary. If the button contain copper, it must be scorified until no more copper can be seen on hammering. If nickel is present the button cannot be cupelled.

3d. CUPELLATION.—This operation differs from scorification in that the scoriæ formed are absorbed by the cupel, leaving a pure bead of the precious metals.

It is thus that we get rid of small amounts of copper, iron, arsenic, etc., in the lead button. The proportion of lead required to carry off impurities, varies according to circumstances. The operation of cupelling is conducted as follows: A cupel is wiped out with the fingers carefully, all extraneous matter blown out, and then placed in the muffle and heated until of the same temperature as the latter, when the button is gently placed in the cupel with a pair of forceps. The muffle is then closed by a door or a piece of lighted charcoal, to melt the lead. This done, the muffle is opened and the button, which at first appears bright and uncovered, is soon coated with a film of oxide moving in luminous patches over its surface, and being continually thrown toward the edge, where it is absorbed by the cupel. The button gradually diminishes in size by oxidation and absorption, and becomes more convex ; the patches become larger and move more quickly ; the last of the lead is absorbed, and the residue appears to revolve rapidly, becomes very brilliant, and is suffused with the tints of the rainbow ; then presents the appearance of the precious metals. The latter part of the operation is called the "brightening" of the button. Should the bead be large and composed of silver, it must be removed slowly from the furnace to prevent "spitting," by which portions of the metal are thrown off and lost. In case the bead is very large, say one hundred to three hundred milligrammes, it is well to cover it with a hot cupel. If the bead is not larger than an ordinary pill, the danger of spitting is slight and no precaution need be taken in its removal.

Two causes have been assigned for this spitting. First, That the molten silver absorbs oxygen from the atmosphere and gives it up at the moment of solidifying. Second, That by rapid cooling a crust is formed upon the outside which contracts upon the liquid interior.

It is well to raise the heat of the muffle just at the time of brightening, or to push the cupel into the hotter part to remove the last traces of lead.

Silver is sensibly volatile at a high heat, and the loss increases with the temperature. We must avoid the two extremes of a high heat and quick work, and a low heat and prolonged work. Of the two the latter is worse. The following are indices of favorable working: The muffle is reddish-white, the cupel red, the fused metal luminous and clear, the lead fumes rise slowly, and the litharge is completely absorbed by the cupel.

The heat is too great when the cupels are whiteish, when the fused metal is seen with difficulty and the scarcely visible fumes rise rapidly.

The heat is too low when the fumes are thick and fall, and when the unabsorbed litharge forms lumps and scales about the button.

The degree of heat may be greater according as the lead is poorer in silver. By bearing this in mind the assayer can often hasten the operation without detriment.

Too strong a current of air cools the cupel and oxidizes the lead faster than it can be absorbed. Too slow a current prolongs the operation, and increases the loss by volatilization.

Sometimes the material in a cupel becomes solidified in the midst of an operation, stopping further action. This is called "freezing," and is occasioned by a production of litharge more rapidly than it can be absorbed by the cupel; infusible scoriæ due to a cold furnace, or an excess of foreign oxides. It can sometimes be remedied by raising the heat of the muffle; or if the accident be due to foreign oxides, an addition of pure lead may be made to the assay. In either case the results are unreliable.

An assay that has passed well, furnishes a bead well rounded, crystalline below, and readily detached from the cupel. If the bead contain lead it is brilliant below, and does not adhere at all to the cupel. If it exhibits rootlets, the results are inaccurate, and must be rejected.

4TH. WEIGHING THE BEAD.—The bead of gold and silver is detached from the cupel with pincers, thoroughly cleansed and weighed.

5TH. INQUARTATION AND PARTING.—The separation of gold from silver is termed parting. It is effected by means of nitric acid, which dissolves the silver and leaves the gold. It is essential that a certain relation should exist between the amount of gold and silver in the alloy.

If there be too little silver it will not dissolve completely but will be so enveloped in the gold as to escape the action of the acid.

If too much silver be present, the gold obtained will be so fine and light as to occasion loss in washing.

The silver should be from two and one-half to three times the weight of gold. The assayer must judge by the color of the bead as to the proportion of silver contained, and if it be too small, he must supply the deficiency with pure silver, which is kept on hand in thin foil. The bead and silver are well fused together to effect complete distribution of the silver. The fusion may be made on charcoal by the blowpipe, or by wrapping the bead and silver in a cornet of lead foil, and cupelling it.

FIG. 27.

The bead is then flattened on an anvil, and treated in a porcelain capsule (Fig. 27), with nitric acid, C. P. 1.16 Sp. gr. (21° Beaumé). Enough acid is added to cover the bead and heated gently. The acid must be free from chlorine, which would precipitate the silver. When all action of the first acid has ceased, decant, and carefully add some fresh acid of 1.26 sp. gr. (32° Beaumé). Heat for several minutes, pour off the acid and wash thoroughly with distilled water, and dry the residue of gold. It is well to apply a high heat before attempting to remove the gold, to render it adherent. The gold residue is detached with a knife, transferred to a cornet of lead, cupelled and weighed. Or if perfectly clean and yellow, weighed without cupellation.

6TH. WEIGHING THE GOLD. — The gold obtained is weighed, as described, and the assay is completed.

CALCULATION OF RESULTS. — The milligrammes of precious metal obtained per assay ton of ore, correspond to Troy ounces in the ton of two thousand pounds avoirdupois. There is therefore no trouble save in the case of an ore which contains metallic scales, and the method employed when such is the case, can be shown by an example. The sample presented for assay weighs 485 gms. Pulverized and sifted it gave:

A. Sifted ore............................480. gms.
B. Metallic scales.......................5. "

There will be a little loss in sifting, but if the operation be done carefully it need not be taken into account.

A. SIFTED ORE.—10 grammes gave by crucible assay:
Gold..4. mgs.
Silver, after deduction of the silver in the litharge, 14.3 "

Hence, the total precious metal in the siftings is:

Gold.................................. $\frac{4.00}{10} \times 480 = 192.0$

Silver................................ $\frac{14.30}{10} \times 480 = 686.4$

B. METALLIC SCALES.—These melted with lead gave a button of, say 60 gms., which was rolled out and 10 gms. taken for cupellation, which yielded:

Gold.................................2.6 mgs.
Silver...............................500.0 "

Hence, the total precious metals in residue must be:

Gold............................ $\frac{2.6}{10}\times 60=$ 15.60 mgs.

Silver............................ $\frac{500.}{10}\times 60=$3000.00 "

Total:

Gold in siftings..............................192.00 mgs.
" " residue.............................. 15.60 "
" " ore taken..............................207.60 "

Hence:

$\frac{207.60}{485}\times 29.166$ (value of an assay ton)=gold per assay ton of original ore.

Silver in total siftings.......................... 686.40 mgs.
" " residue..............................3000.00 "
" " ore taken..............................3686.40 "

Hence:

$\frac{3686.40}{485}\times 29.166$ (value of an assay ton)=silver per assay ton of original ore.

REMARKS.—All ores or minerals of gold or silver can be assayed by either (*a*) crucible, or (*b*) scorification. The latter is preferable whenever it can be used, as it yields higher results and requires no preliminary assay. No oxy-sulphurets are formed, or if formed, are decomposed during the operation; whereas, in the crucible assay they may escape decomposition even at a white heat. It is a better method for copper ores, the action of scorification being oxidizing, that of the crucible reducing; in the latter case much copper will enter the lead button that, in the former, would be oxidized and enter the slag. Instead of roasting, a good method for arsenical and antimonial ores is, ore 1 A. T., litharge 2 A. T, soda 1 A. T, ferro-cyanide of potassium 35 gms., and a cover of salt. The button must be scorified. The matte over the button should be saved and put in the scorifier.

After roasting an ore for crucible assay, if much iron is contained, add more charcoal than is necessay for a fifteen gm. button, as the ore has an oxydizing action. Sometimes, to avoid roasting, just sufficient litharge may be added to give the required button of lead, but this is not always safe. Alloys which contain gold and silver may be fused in a scorifier with pure lead, and the button scorified down and cupelled, the resulting bead being carefully parted with nitric acid in the usual way. In weighing the gold which has been parted, if not previously cupelled, it can be transferred to the scale-pan by means of a piece of pointed wood, great care being observed not to lose any.

The assay of gold and silver, if conducted carefully, is one of great accuracy. Duplicates of silver should agree to within one-half ounce Troy per ton of two thousand pounds, and for gold there should be no difference. This is true of all ores, though some are more difficult than others. Where the difference is greater than the above and accuracy is required, a third assay should be made. Tests made in duplicate of type ores gave:

ORE.	SILVER.	GOLD.
Gold ore, quartzose....29.	and 29.2 ozs.	10.4 and 10.4 ozs.
Poor Galena.......... 5.4	" 5.4 "	none
Zinc Blende.......... 4.3	" 4.3 "	"
Arsenical............55.	" 55. "	trace
Antimonial..........57.	" 57. "	none
Impure mixture......28.6	" 28.6 "	2.4 and 2.4 ozs.

PLATINUM. *Symbol*—Pt.

SOURCES.—Platinum is found native and associated with a variety of metals, such as palladium, iridium, osmium, copper, iron, gold, silver, etc.

It occurs in alluvial deposits in grains, and sometimes in masses.

ASSAY.—The assay of platinum may be performed in two ways:

(*a*). By fusion with lead. (*b*). By solution and precipitation. (See scheme, p. 108).

(*a*). Fusion with lead: Weigh and pulverize the sample as finely as possible, and sift; the metallic residue will contain most of the metal sought for. Weigh the residue and siftings separately.

1. Siftings—charge 20 gms. in a small crucible with

Litharge	50 gms.
Borax glass	15 "
Soda	30 "
Charcoal	1 "

Part of the soda should be mixed with the charge and part used as a cover. The proportion of fluxes may be varied to suit the gangue, so as to render the slag as fusible as possible.

The litharge is reduced by the charcoal and alloys with the platinum and foreign metals, save osm-iridium, which will be found principally under the lead button. The lead button is then broken out, scorified with a little borax glass if too large, and cupelled at as high a temperature as possible in an ordinary bone-ash cupel until it solidifies. The residue will be platinum, with a little silver, gold, etc. It may be purified by fusing in a crucible of cut lime, which is heated by coal gas, the combustion being supported by a current of oxygen.

The lead retained in the unpurified button is about one-eighth to one-fourth of its weight.

2. Residue—Fuse directly in a scorifier, with pure lead and borax glass, cupelling the whole or a weighed portion of the resulting button if it be too large, as in 1.

REMARKS.—In place of the method used for the siftings, pure galena and iron wire might be employed, as in the assay for lead, other fluxes being added to suit.

In the charge given for siftings, twenty to thirty grammes of granulated lead in addition to the litharge, can be used with advantage.

Instead of cupelling the lead button containing the platinum alone, add five to six times the weight of the platinum in silver. This gives a result free from lead. The silver can afterwards be deducted in the calculation of the platinum.

ZINC. *Symbol*—Zn.

SOURCES.—The principal ores of zinc are:

Blende, sulphide (ZnS)	67.7	pure zinc
Smithsonite, carbonate ($ZnCO_3$)	52.	" "
Calamine, silicate ($Zn2SiO_3$)	53.8	" "
Zincite, oxide (ZnO)	80.26	" "

The latter occurs in Franklinite.

The ores are found alone or associated with the ores of other metals; this being especially true of the sulphide in the case of silver and lead.

ASSAY.—The assay for zinc is attended with considerable difficulty, and is not accurate save when done in the wet way (See scheme, p. 109); zinc being volatile and easily oxidized. The amount of zinc may be estimated pretty closely by the following method, when no lead or antimony are present.

Weigh out 10 gms. of the finely pulverized ore and roast it carefully, with the addition of a little carbonate of ammonia, to decompose any sulphates formed. Weigh and mix the residue with

Kaolin, or fire clay (dry)....................1 gm.
Lime, " ....5 "

and charge the mixture in a charcoal-lined crucible, as in the iron assay, but not luting on the cover tight. Fuse at as high a temperature as possible for about two and one-half to three hours. Cool, and break the crucible open. The zinc will have been reduced and expelled. The residue, consisting of slag, and metallic globules if much iron was present in the ore, should be weighed and powdered. Separate the globules with the magnet, weigh them, and add three-tenths of their weight to that of the total residue for the oxygen lost by reduction. The total weight thus obtained deducted from that of the roasted ore and fluxes charged, and the difference multiplied by $\frac{16.3}{20.3}$ gives the yield of metallic zinc.

REMARKS.—The kind and amount of fluxes used depends upon the character of the gangue of the ore treated; fusible ores not requiring any.

The factors used to calculate the amount of oxygen and the metallic zinc are deduced from the table of combining weights. (Page 14).

The method given is not applicable to ores where zinc blende is associated with sulphide of lead, antimony, arsenic, etc., and carries gold and silver. The latter metals would be reduced and go into the buttons of iron, causing error in the calculation of the oxygen to be added. The method for practical purposes may prove sufficiently close, but where accuracy is required the wet method for zinc is preferable, and is recommended

MERCURY. *Symbol*—Hg.

SOURCES.—The principal ore of mercury is cinnabar (sulphide) (HgS), =86.27 when pure. It also occurs in the metallic state, alone and amalgated with silver, gold, etc., and is sometimes found combined with chlorine.

ASSAY.—The determination of mercury is made by distillation.

1. Ore, sulphide and chloride.

Charge—Ore finely pulverized....................10 gms.
Black flux substitute..................15 "

This should be mixed by rubbing together with water and drying. The dried mixture being charged in an iron, glass or clay retort, with a bent neck, the end of which is plunged in a glass vessel, to collect the distilled metal. It is better also to wrap the neck of the retort with a damp cloth. The retort may be heated over a small charcoal furnace, or in any way by which the heat can be applied slowly, and the whole body of the retort heated, to prevent condensation of the mercury on the top. When after heating some time, no more mercury comes over, the end of the neck should be lifted out of the water to prevent its being drawn over into the retort. The latter is allowed to cool slowly; and all adhering particles of the metal are brushed with a feather into the glass receiver, where they can be collected by boiling the water for a moment. The water is then decanted, and the mercury dried at the ordinary temperature or with blotting paper, and weighed on glass. Sometimes lime or iron filings are used in place of an alkaline flux; the object being, however, in any case, to decompose the mercurial compound, freeing that metal, the substance used taking up the sulphur and chlorine. The determinations must be made in duplicate, and for very poor ores, the pulverized sample should be first digested in muriatic and nitric acids (aqua regia); the solution filtered off and evaporated to dryness, and the dried mass treated by distillation, as described.

2. Metallic mercury and amalgams.

Distill without the addition of any decomposing agent, otherwise conducting the operation as above. The heat used need not be so high, mercury being very volatile.

Remarks.—For all distillations the retort should be tight. For this reason glass or iron retorts are the best. Earthen retorts should be glazed.

Care should be taken not to inhale any of the fumes.

See Mitchell—page 453, and Goodyear's translation of Bodeman and Kerl, page 207.

The wet method is preferable for mercury ores.

BISMUTH. *Symbol*—Bi.

Sources.—This metal is found principally in the metallic state, but it also occurs in combination with sulphur, oxygen and tellurium, associated with lead and silver. Bismuth possesses equally with lead the property of causing the absorption of the metallic oxides in cupellation, and may be used in place of the latter, but is not recommended.

ASSAY.—In the assay for bismuth three cases may occur.

a. The sample contains native bismuth.

b. The sample is composed of bismuth with other substances, or bismuth residue.

c. The sample is an alloy.

a. Determine as in the assay for "antimonium crudum," the bismuth being collected in the same way.

b. Pulverize finely and charge

Ore	10 gms.
Borax glass	25 "
Soda	10 "
Cyanide of potassium	6 "
Salt	cover

Fuse in a moderate fire in the same manner as for antimony. The resulting button must be tested for other metals, and if any be present treated as an alloy.

c. Determine by the wet assay. (See scheme, page 111).

REMARKS.—Bismuth melts at 260° F., and is volatile at a higher temperature.

The assay for bismuth may also be made by fusing the pulverized and sintered ore (prepared by heating alone in a closed crucible) with a known weight, (five to ten gms.) of fine silver, black flux, and three to five gms. of iron wire, covering with salt. The button can afterward be treated as an alloy. Plattner's Manual of Blowpipe Analysis, page 459.

A button of bismuth should not be hammered, as it is brittle.

TIN. *Symbol*—Sn.

SOURCES.—The most abundant ore is cassiterite (binoxide) (SnO_2), =78.67 per cent. when pure. It is found in veins and in the washings from the same under the name of stream tin; sometimes it is associated with tungsten, tantalum, or molybdenum. Tin also occurs as a sulphide in stanite (tin pyrites $\left\{\begin{matrix} Cu_2S \\ FeS \end{matrix}\right\} SnS_2$)=14.30 per cent. tin, and rarely in the native state.

ASSAY.—The treatment of tin ores in the laboratory is a matter of some difficulty for several reasons:

1st. The ore is often associated with a gangue, the constituents of which either form salts with the oxide of tin or alloy with the reduced metal from the same.

2d. The majority of the basic fluxes at the disposal of the assayer combine with the tin and oxygen which may be present, forming stannates which go into the slag.

3d. Acid fluxes, especially silica, form compounds with the oxide of tin, and carry it into the slag. The influence of silica can be seen by the following table, given by Mitchell. The last line shows the yield of metal:

Ore........	10.00	10.00	10.00	10.00	10.00 gms.
Silica......	2.50	6.60	10.00	15.00	30.00 "
Tin........	52%	43%	28%	10%	none

The fusion being made in each case with an equal quantity of black flux.

4th. Binoxide of tin is extremely difficult to fuse; it is insoluble even in concentrated acids, and although it is reducible by ignition with hydrogen, charcoal, etc., there is always danger of loss if the temperature be too high, as tin boils and volatilizes at a white heat, air being excluded.

The various methods adopted for the assay of tin may be divided into four classes:

a. For pure binoxide of tin.

b. For ore containing silica only.

c. For very impure ores, sulphides, etc.

d. For alloys from the dry assay or tin buttons.

a. Treatment of the pure binoxide.

1. Charge ten gms. of ore finely pulverized, into a charcoal-lined crucible, lute the cover well on, then heat for twenty-five minutes, raising the heat gradually until it is almost white. Remove the crucible from the fire but do not tap it. If the tin be in small globules, pulverize in a mortar, and pass through a fine sieve to separate from the charcoal. This method gives good results if the ore be perfectly pure, but not otherwise.

2. Ore....................................10 gms.
Cyanide of potassium........40 "

Use a chalk-lined crucible, one-half of the cyanide being placed in the bottom of the crucible, and the rest mixed with the ore. Cover with cyanide and then with salt; fuse for ten minutes in a good fire, withdraw, cool, break and weigh. For binoxide and pure ores containing little silica, this method gives excellent results.

Foreign metals may be removed before fusion by the process given on page 112, or the button may be treated as an alloy.

b. Ores containing silica only.

1. Ore....................................10 gms.
Fluor spar or cryolite....10 to 20 "

Mix well and charge in a charcoal-lined crucible, which is first covered with charcoal and then luted with clay. Heat strongly for about one hour. Remove carefully from the fire without tapping. Treat the button as an alloy afterwards.

2. Ore........................10 gms.
Hematite..................3 to 8 "
Cyanide of potassium........40 "

Mix and charge in a charcoal-lined crucible, cover with cyanide, and then with charcoal, lute and heat strongly from one-half to one hour; remove without tapping, cool, and break. If the tin be in small buttons, collect by washing with water to separate the charcoal, dry and weigh. Treat the button as an alloy of tin and iron.

3. Ore........................10 gms.
Oxide of copper.............10 "
Black flux substitute.........25 "
Borax glass................. 5 "

Mix, and cover with salt and charcoal in a chalk-lined crucible. Heat gradually and finally to a white heat for one hour. Tap, cool and weigh. Treat the button as an alloy of copper and tin. Mitchell, page 411.

4. Ore........................10 gms.
Black flux substitute.........25 "
Chloride of silver (dry)........10 "
Starch........................ 5 "
Borax glass.................. 5 "
Salt........................ cover

Use a chalk-lined crucible, and a hot fire. Treat the button as an alloy.

c. Very impure ores, sulphides, etc. Weigh out and roast carefully, first alone and then with a little charcoal, to remove arsenic and antimony, adding finally carbonate of ammonia to decompose sulphates; then treat by any method for ores containing silica. Testing the button for iron, etc., or after roasting separate all associated metals by the method on page 112, and then fuse for tin.

d. Alloys—As tin fuses at 228° F., it may be roughly separated from iron and metals of a less degree of fusibility, by simply heating the alloy so that the melted tin can drain off. The only true way, however, is to treat by the wet method, page 115.

REMARKS. — The method by fusion with cryolite or fluor spar can be performed in a small charcoal-lined crucible, with two gms. of finely pulverized and well mixed ore; the crucible being luted and placed in a cupel muffle.

The time required is about one-half hour, the muffle being filled with charcoal the last fifteen minutes, the door closed, and as high a heat obtained as possible.

Assays of Durango tin ore containing silica, by the above methods, gave the following average results:

METHOD-	TIN FOUND.
a—2	67.0 per cent.
b—1	75.4 " "
b—2	74.0 " "
b—3	67.1 " "
b—4	61.7 " "

b—1 and *b*—2 seem to be the only methods by which the tin is entirely reduced.

COPPER. *Symbol*—Cu.

SOURCES.—The substances containing copper may be divided into three classes:

1st. Pure or oxidized ores.

2d. Impure ores, or compounds of copper and other metals, with sulphur, arsenic, antimony, etc.

3d. Native copper and alloys.

The most abundant being native copper and its silver alloy.

Cuprite (red oxide) (Cu_2O), ...	=88.7	when pure.
Malachite (carbonate) ($CuCO_3.CuH_2O_2$), ...	=57.3	" "
Azurite (blue carbonate) ($2CuCO_3.CuH_2O_2$),	=55.	" "
Chalcocite (copper glance) (Cu_2S), ...	=79.8	" "
Chalcopyrite (copper pyrites) ($Cu_2S.Fe_2S_3$),	=34.4	" "
Erubescite (purple copper) ($3Cu_2S.Fe_2S_3$),	=55.7	" "

Compounds with arsenic, antimony, lead, mercury, etc., and the chloride, atacamite.

ASSAY.—Weigh out ten gms. of the ore and roast it carefully; if it contains sulphur, arsenic, etc., with three times its volume of fine charcoal or two or three grammes of fine pure graphite. If the ore be very fusible add five grammes of powdered hematite, mix the charge well before roasting, and line the pan or vessel with chalk or oxide of iron. Add carbonate of ammonia toward the end to decompose sulphates. After roasting mix the ore with

Black flux, substitute.............	20 gms.
Borax glass......................	3 "
Hematite (peroxide of iron)	10 to 20 "

Cover with a mixture of ten gms. black flux substitue and three gms. charcoal, then with salt. Fuse in an ordinary chalk-lined crucible for twenty minutes. When perfectly fused, pour carefully into a mould.

The resulting copper button must be refined by fusing it as quickly as possible in a shallow dish in the cupel muffle. with an equal weight of borax or less, and a little pure lead;

one to five grammes will generally be sufficient; and if the ore contains lead, its addition is unnecessary. When the copper is nearly refined it brightens somewhat like silver, only less distinctly, showing a peculiar green color. If the button is small, the assay is considered finished when it no longer fumes.

Instead of the above the following charge may be used in fusing.

Ore	10	gms.
Black flux substitute	20	"
Borax glass	5	"
Litharge	8	"

Mix well and cover with salt and charcoal. Then refine as described. The action in the crucible is reducing. An alloy of copper and other metals, if present, being formed which must be refined.

REMARKS.—A good refining flux is

Nitre	3	pts.
Argol	2½	"
Salt	1	"

Fuse together, pulverize, sift through a thirty-mesh sieve, and test its action on a piece of copper before using.

Iron prevents loss of copper in the slag, which is always the case, when the latter has a red color, due to the suboxide of copper. If the button from the crucible is small the best way is to refine it before the blowpipe on charcoal, with a little boracic acid, blowing on the slag only, after the assay is once fused.

It is better to determine copper ores by the wet method, and in case silver, gold, etc., be present, they must be treated in this way. (See scheme 115).

The dry assay is only approximate owing to the loss of copper in the slag, but if care be taken fair results may be obtained.

Copper can also be determined by roasting the ore with carbonate of ammonia and then fusing with arsenic and slagging off the other arsenides combined with it, as described in the nickel and cobalt assay. This method is exact but difficult of execution, but it serves to determine besides the copper; lead, bismuth, cobalt, and nickel. Watts' Dictionary of Chemistry, Vol. II, page 63. The crucible used for the fusion is shown in Fig. 28. The operation is conducted in the muffle furnace.

Fig. 28.

IRON. *Symbol*—Fe.

Sources.—The following is a list of the principal ores of iron.

Ore		
Magnetic iron ore (oxide) (Fe_3O_4), ...	=72.41	when pure
Red hematite or specular iron (oxide) (Fe_2O_3), ...	=70.00	" "
Brown hematite or limonite (oxide)($2Fe_2O_3.3H_2O$), ...	=59.92	" "
Spathic iron ore (carbonate) ($FeCO_3$),....	=48.22	" "
Ilmenite (titaniferous ore) ($FeTiO_3+nFe_2O_3$), ...	=36.82	" "
Franklinite $3(FeO.ZnO.MnO)+(Fe_2O_3.Mn_2O_3)$, ...	=45.16	" "

Assay.—It is required in the assay for iron to reduce the oxide to cast-iron, collect the latter in a button, and to form a fusible slag that will not retain any of the iron in combination or in pellets. The oxide is reduced by carbon, and we employ for this purpose crucibles lined with brasque, which has a composition of four parts finely pulverized charcoal to one of molasses. (To prepare this, see page 26).

The lining serves as a support for the crucible, which, under the high heat, is apt to soften.

In making up the charge we may have, (1), Ores of unknown composition, and (2), Ores previously analyzed. The assay in both cases gives a clue to the nature of the slag, the iron that may be obtained from the ore, and the character and proportion of the fluxes to be added in the blast furnace. In the first case we obtain the additional information of the approximate percentage of iron.

1. Ores of unknown composition.

In the assay of an ore the composition of which is unknown, we make several preliminary assays, and if satisfactory results are obtained we make another assay with a charge modified according to the indications of the best preliminary assay.

Preliminary assay charges :

	1.	2.	3.	4.	
Silica	2.5	1.	4.0	2.5 to 0.	gms.
Lime	2.5	4.	1.0	2.5 to 3.	"
Ore	10.0	10.	10.0	10.0	"

1 is employed for the purer ores containing very little gangue; 2, for ores containing silica; 3, for ores containing the carbonates of lime, magnesia, protoxide of manganese, etc.; calcareous hematites and spathic iron; 4, for ores containing silica and alumina; clay iron stones, black band, etc.

The principle involved is that of furnishing a base for an acid, and *vice versa*. The charge, therefore, depends upon the acid or basic nature of the gangue of the ore.

Ores containing titanium require the addition of fluorspar in the charge in quantity varying from 0.5 to 10 gms.

2. Ores previously analyzed.

Good results are obtained from a charge proportioned to yield a slag corresponding to a blast furnace cinder, having the composition $R_2O_3.SiO_2+2(3RO.SiO_2)$.

R_2O_3 represents alumina, and RO, lime, magnesia, and other bases. Its approximate percentage composition is as follows:

Silica	38.	or about	2½ parts.
R_2O_3 (alumina)	15.		1 "
RO. (lime, magnesia, etc.)	47.		3 "

The method of charging can best be shown by example.

The Ore contains	Per Cent.	10 gms. of ore contains	Slag required.	Difference to be added.
Silica	1.65	0.165	2.50	2.335 gms.
Alumina	1.94	0.194	1.00	0.806 "
Lime, magnesia, etc.	4.51	0.451	3.00	2.549 "

The alumina is added in the form of kaolin or fire-clay, which contains nearly equal parts of alumina and silica. Allow in adding silica for that introduced in the kaolin.

Sometimes the ore contains more than one of the ingredients of the slag, or the silica introduced with the kaolin may, when added to that already present, increase the quantity beyond the requirement. In either case make up a new slag with the excess, retaining the same proportion between the silica, alumina and lime, viz: silica, 2½; alumina, 1; lime, 3.

The charge should be thoroughly mixed, placed in the crucible, the conical cavity closed with a piece of charcoal, and the whole top of the crucible covered with a luting of fire-clay. The latter is mixed with one-fourth to one-third part of fine sand and made plastic with borax water.

Four crucibles are introduced in the furnace luted to a fire-brick, and a low fire kindled around them. The fuel is added gradually until it is above the tops of the crucibles; the fire is maintained at its maximum temperature for two and one-half to three and one-half hours. Ores containing much titanium require four hours, while carbonates containing manganese, fuse well in two and one-half hours, or even less time. When the fire has burned out the bricks and crucibles are removed in one mass, the crucibles detached and their exteriors broken with a hammer; on inverting and tapping the charcoal lining the slag and button of cast-iron will fall into the hand. If they adhere together, a slight tap will serve to separate them.

Before separation they should be carefully cleansed and weighed, the slag may then be broken, and any particles of iron separated with a magnet.

Titanium and manganese enter the slag almost completely. Duplicate assays should not differ more than 0.3 to 0.4 of one per cent. The slag ought to be well fused and free from iron. A good button is well formed and detached from the slag.

If the metal be of good quality the button will flatten slightly before breaking. It ought to be gray or grayish white, and the grain fine.

A button of bad iron breaks readily without changing form.

Transparent slags of a greenish tint indicate excess of silica. A rough, stony slag, or one crystalline in structure, and dull in lustre indicates an excess of bases. If the product is only fritted and contains the reduced iron interspersed as a fine grey powder, silica and alumina are deficient in the flux, lime and magnesia being in excess.

The latter base is one of the most refractory found in iron ores, and when present in quantity requires an addition of both silica and lime.

Manganese gives an amethystine tint to the slag, or if in excess a yellow, green or brown color.

Titanium produces a resinous, black, scoriacious slag, curiously wrinkled on the outside, and covered with metallic pelicles of nitro-cyanide of titanium with its characteristic copper color; sometimes the slag is vitreous and of a bluish tint.

Chromium gives a dark resinous slag surrounded with a thin metallic coating.

Phoshorus gives a hard, brittle, white metal; what is known as cold short.

Sulphur a strong, reticulated, mottled structure, and red short iron.

Manganese, a button smooth on the exterior, hard and non-graphitic; it presents a white crystalline fracture.

Titanium—The button is smooth on the outside; has a deep gray fracture, dull and crystalline; and adheres strongly to the slag. The button is sometimes covered with the nitro-cyanide of titanium with its characteristic copper color.

Chromium—The button is smooth, well fused, with a brilliant crystalline fracture, and tin-white color; at other times it is white and only half fused, or it may even form a spongy mass of a clear gray color, according to the quantity of chromium contained in the iron.

REMARKS.—A number of type ores gave on assay:

Ore.	Iron by Analysis.	By Fire Assay.			
Magnetite.....	68.35 per cent.	69.6	71.2	71.3	per cent.
Hematite......	44.50 "	44.6	46.0	48.6	"
Limonite......	44,20 "	44.3	44.6	45.2	"

Assays of magnetite containing titanic acid gave 72.5 and 73. per cent.

Another magnetite	64.0	64.5 per cent.
Hematite	39.0	38.5 "
Limonite	34.0	34.0 "

Other slags besides the ones given might be used, as Bodemans, which is silica 56, lime 30, alumina 14 per cent. An addition of borax and fluorspar makes this more fluid.

NICKEL AND COBALT. *Symbols*—Ni. and Co.

SOURCES.—These two metals are generally found associated, and their treatment will be described under the same head.

The principal ore of nickel is niccolite (copper nickel) (Ni_2As)=43 to 50 per cent.

The principal ore of cobalt is smaltine (tin-white cobalt) ($CoAs_2$)=24 to 33 per cent.

Both nickel and cobalt occur in many other minerals, chiefly in combination with sulphur or arsenic, and associated with iron, copper, lead, etc.

We have also an artificial product called "spiess," which is an arsenide of cobalt, nickel and iron, obtained in the smelting of ores which contain nickel and cobalt, and in the manufacture of smalt (cobalt glass).

ASSAY.—Cobalt and nickel being difficult to fuse they are determined in combination with arsenic. Weigh out from two to five grammes according to the purity of the ore, roast thoroughly in the muffle, using a clay roasting dish, and mixing with six to ten grammes of fine charcoal toward the last of the operation. When the sample has ceased to evolve an odor, mix thoroughly with one to five gms. carbonate of ammonia and heat. The resulting oxides are then converted into arsenides by mixing with one to five gms. metallic arsenic, (according to the amount of ore taken), placed in a small clay crucible (Fig. 28), which will stand in the muffle, and heated, keeping at a dull red until the fumes of arsenic have ceased; when the crucible is removed and six to thirty gms. of black flux, or its substitute added, with a covering of salt. Do not mix the flux, but place it over the mass in the crucible; after which heat in a good fire, raising the temperature gradually, until the contents of the crucible are in a quiet state of fusion. Make the heat strong toward the end of the operation, but be careful not to let the charge boil over. Cool and break the crucible, remove and weigh the button (*a*) of arsenides of cobalt, nickel, iron, copper, etc. The rest of the process consists in scorifying the button, first, to remove the iron, and afterwards to separate the nickel and cobalt. This can be done in a shallow dish, or on a piece of clay crucible about two inches long by one inch wide, and slightly concave; in the cupel muffle, which should be pretty hot and contain a piece of glowing charcoal in front. Place on the dish the button of arsenides from the fusion and cover it with borax glass. Introduce it into the muffle and close the latter until the button and borax are fused, then allow air to enter. The arsenide of iron will oxidize first and go into the slag, and the surface of the button will become bright, when the dish should be removed immediately placed upon the surface of a basin of water until the button solidifies, and then immersed. If the slag shows a slight blue color the iron is entirely removed and the button may be cleaned and weighed. (*b*).

If the desired purity from iron is not obtained by one scorification repeat the operation, weighing the button each time. Should the button become bright immediately, showing that little or no iron was contained, take the previous weight. The button will consist of arsenide of nickel, cobalt and copper (Ni_2As. Co_2As. Cu_6As_2).

Next slag off the cobalt in the same manner as the iron. This operation must be continued until an apple-green film forms, which will float about on the surface of the button. Weigh the button (*c*).

If copper is present add 100 to 500 milligrammes of gold (weighed), and then proceed to slag off the nickel with the addition of a little salt of phosphorus, conducting the operation as before, until the button shows the bluish-green color peculiar to gold and copper when melted. Weigh the alloy of copper and gold (*d*).

To determine the weight of copper, subtract the weight of gold added from the last button. The difference will be the metallic copper. To determine the weight of nickel, multiply the weight of the copper by $\frac{100}{71.7}$, this will give the arsenide of copper (Cu_6As_2), which, subtracted from the weight (*c*), will give the arsenide of nickel. This multipled by $\frac{60.7}{100}$=the nickel. To determine the cobalt subtract the weight (*c*) from (*b*) and multiply by $\frac{61.5}{100}$

The results thus obtained divided by the weight of ore taken for assay and multiplied by 100 gives the percentage in each case.

REMARKS.—Results compare well with the battery process. Composition of the arsenides:

Ni_2As	Cu_6As_2	Co_2As
As=28.31 per ct.	As=39.27 per ct.	As=38.46 per ct.
Cu=71.69 "	Ni=60.73 "	Co=61.54 "

When the ore treated contains bismuth and lead in any quantity these metals can be separated during the fusion with black flux by adding one gm. of iron wire, and one to three gms. of pure silver, accurately weighed. After fusion the lead and bismuth will be found alloyed with the silver, and can be detached without trouble from the arsenides. By deducting the silver, the lead and bismuth may be determined. When the substance treated is poor in nickel and cobalt, it is well to add some collecting agent in the fusion. Arsenide of iron is the best for this purpose; it may be prepared by fusing iron filings with metallic arsenic in a crucible.

CARBON. *Symbol—C.*

Sources.—Carbon occurs in a vast number of compounds forming, with hydrogen, oxygen, and nitrogen, an immense series of organic substances; but only the following are of interest to the assayer:

Diamond, pure carbon..........................crystallized.
Graphite, nearly pure...................95—100 per cent.
Anthracite...............................90— 95 "
Bituminous coal.......................... variable
Peat and lignite..........................about 60 per ct.
Charcoal................................ variable

Assay.—The assay of a specimen of coal varies with the purpose for which the coal is to be employed. The most general tests are: Determination of moisture, specific gravity, heating power, volatile products, coke, ash, and in some cases sulphur and phosphorus.

The moisture, volatile products, coke, and ash may be determined by the schemes given below. The specific gravity by formulæ, pages 138-139. Knowing the elementary constitution of the fuel, the heating power may be tested by determining the amount of oxygen required to burn it.

Charge—1 gm. of powdered coal, and 50 gms. of litharge, well mixed, in a crucible, and cover with 20 gms. of litharge. Heat gradually until fusion is complete. The time required will be about ten minutes. Cool and break the crucible, then weigh the button of lead. Pure carbon should reduce thirty-four times its own weight of lead. Hydrogen 103.7 times its weight. Instead of litharge, white lead may be used, the proportion being one gm. of coal to seventy gms. of white lead, and thirty gms. of the same for a cover. If the white lead be pure it is better than litharge.

To calculate the results, compare with the amount of oxygen consumed in burning a fuel whose calorific power is known. One part of pure carbon can raise the temperature of 8080 parts of water 1°. Consequently the value of the fuel in units of heat may be estimated by multiplying $\frac{8080}{34}$ by the weight of the lead button obtained in the assay. When much hydrogen is present in the fuel the method is not so accurate. The specific colorific effect of a fuel may be estimated by multiplying the absolute effect by the specific gravity of the fuel.

To determine moisture, volatile and combustible matter, fixed carbon (coke), ash, and sulphur.

a. Determination of moisture. Pulverize the coal finely, heat one to two gms in a covered platinum or porcelain crucible fifteen minutes, in an air bath at 212° to 240° F. Cool and weigh, repeat until weight is constant, or begins to rise. Loss=moisture.

b. Determination of volatile and combustible matter. Heat the same crucible with contents to bright redness over a Bunsen burner or alcohol lamp, exactly three and one-half minutes, and then three and one-half minutes over a blast lamp. Cool and weigh. Loss=volatile and combustible matter. This also includes one-half the sulphur from any sulphide of iron contained in the coal.

c. Fixed carbon. Heat over the burner until the ash is white and constant in weight. Loss=fixed carbon and one-half the sulphur from the sulphide of iron.

The sulphur must be determined by the wet method, page 122. For phosphorus, see Fresenius on Quantitative Analysis.

REMARKS.—In reporting an analysis of a coal, deduct the sulphur as mentioned, and enter it as a separate item in the analysis, so that it will add up correctly. Any phosphorus present will be contained in the ash ; if determined, allow for it.

To determine the actual volatile matter for gas making purposes, a very rough but simple plan is to heat a small sample in an ordinary clay pipe, luteing the top of the bowl, so that the volatile products will pass out through the stem, at the end of which the gas can be lighted.

Analysis of two samples of different semi-bituminous coal gave the following results :

Moisture	3.310	0.965
Volatile combustible matter	27.300	30.111
Fixed carbon	61.965	61.033
Ash	7.425	7.829
Sulphur	3.863	1.347

27.300 minus $\frac{3.863}{2}$ and 30.111 minus $\frac{1.347}{2}$ gives the correct amount of volatile matter.

61.965 minus $\frac{3.863}{2}$ and 61.033 minus $\frac{1.347}{2}$ the correct amount of fixed carbon.

Phosphorus not determined.

PART III.

ASSAYS IN THE WET WAY, OR ANALYSES.

SILVER BULLION.

This process embraces two steps:

a. Preliminary assay. *b.* Assay proper.

The latter requires for its conduct, three solutions, called normal salt, decime salt, and decime silver.

The normal salt is a solution of salt 100 c.c. of which will precipitate exactly 1 gm. of silver.

The decime salt is a solution one-tenth the strength of of the normal. One c.c. will precipitate one milligramme of silver; it is made by diluting one part of the normal solution with nine parts of pure water.

The decime silver is a solution of one gm. of pure silver in nitric acid diluted to a litre. One c.c. of this solution will contain one milligramme of pure silver. One c.c. decime silver is equivalent to one c.c. decime salt.

Preparation of the Normal Salt Solution.—A large quantity of the solution is prepared and preserved in common glass carboy, which has affixed to it a paper scale, carefully graduated, indicating its contents at any time It is made by diluting 2.07 parts of a saturated solution of salt with 97.93 parts of pure water, or until each 100 c.c. of the resulting solution contains just .54167 of a gramme of salt, which is the amount necessary to precipitate one gm. of pure silver. The amount of concentrated solution required for 100 c.c. of the normal, depends upon its strength, which can be determined by evaporating a measured portion to dryness, and weighing it. The water and salt solution must be well mixed and the tubes and pipette washed out by allowing some to run through them. The solution must then be tested and accurately standardized. For this purpose three or four solutions of silver in nitric acid are prepared, called check assays, each containing one gm. pure silver. The solutions are made with strong acid in glass stoppered bottles of 8 ozs. or 250 c.c. capacity. Prepare also a temporary decime salt solution by diluting 25 c.c. of the approximate normal with 225 c.c. of water. Run into one of the check assays 100 c.c. of the normal, agitate and allow the precipitated chloride of silver to settle. Repeat the agitation if necessary until the solution settles clear and bright, add now one c.c. of the decime salt solution. Agitate as before, add again one c.c. of the decime salt, and repeat until a precipitate fails to appear. Suppose we have added altogether 14 c.c., the last produced no precipitate and is not counted. Thus 101.3 parts of the normal solution are necessary to precipitate one gramme of silver, while only 100 should be required. The normal is too weak, and the quantity of salt solution to be added may be found by dividing the mumber of c.c. of concentrated salt solution used to make the normal by 100 —1.3 or 98.7, and multiplying by 13, the number of decime added after correction. The solution is again tested, a new decime salt made, and so on. If the normal be too strong calculate from the silver precipitate the excess of salt in the whole solution, and water in the ratio prescribed to dissolve it. C=excess of silver precipitated over 1 gm, hence 1 is to C as .54167 is to 7=salt in excess in 100 c.c. of the normal. This, multiplied by the number of c.c. left, gives the total salt in excess.

a. Preliminary Assay.—This is rendered necessary by the fact of our employing a constant volume of normal salt solution corresponding to one gm. of pure silver.

Weigh out one gramme of the alloy, and wrap it in pure lead foil, which should be kept in small sheets about two inches square, weighing $\frac{17}{100}$ oz.; or 5.287 gms. each, and cupel. Suppose we obtain a button of silver weighing 3.8695 gms., then,—1 is to 0.8695 as 100 is to x=869.5, approximate fineness. The following table from Mitchell gives the corrections to be made. They are in thousandths, and are to be added to the standard:

STANDARD.	CORRECTION.	STANDARD.	CORRECTION.	STANDARD.	CORRECTION.
998.97	1.03	670.27	4.73	346.73	3.27
973.24	1.76	645.29	4.71	322.06	2.94
947.50	2.50	620.30	4.70	297.40	2.60
921.75	3.25	595.32	4.68	272.42	2.58
896.00	4.00	570.32	4.68	247.44	2.56
870.93	4.07	545.32	4.68	222.45	2.55
845.85	4.13	520.32	4.68	197.47	2.55
820.78	4.22	495.32	4.68	173.88	2.12
795.70	4.30	470.50	4.50	148.30	1.70
770.59	4.41	445.69	4.31	123.71	1.29
745.38	4.52	420.87	4.13	99.12	0.88
720.36	4.64	396.05	3.95	74.34	0.66
695.25	4.75	371.39	3.61	49.56	0.44

Example. The number in the column of standards nearest to 869.5 is 870.93; the corresponding correction is 4.07; adding this to 869.5, we obtain 873.57 for the true approximate fineness.

b. ASSAY PROPER.—Take such a weight of alloy as will contain one gm. of pure silver. This is found from the approximate fineness by the following proportion: 873.57 is to 1000 as 1 is to x=1.145 gms. Place this in a glass-stoppered bottle of about 8 oz. capacity, and dissolve in 10 c.c. nitric acid. Heat gently on the sand bath to facilitate solution, and cool. Add 100 c.c. of the normal solution, and proceed in the same way as in testing the normal solution until the decime salt fails to give a precipitate. Suppose we have added 6 c.c. of the decime salt; the last gave no precipitate ; so that we required more than 4 and less than 5, or 4.5 c.c. If greater accuracy be necessary check with the decime silver solution. We have used 100.45 of salt solution=1.0045 gms. of silver. The fineness is given by the following proportion : 1.145 is to 1.0045 as 1000 is to x= the fineness.

Fig. 29.

APPARATUS EMPLOYED.—(Fig. 29). The carboy should hold about 60 litres or 15 to 16 gallons, and have a paper scale affixed to it ; graduated by adding successively a known number of litres of water until the carboy is filled, and marking after each addition the height of the liquid. B and V are parts of a valve. B is the cover of glass through which the tubes pass, fitted by a cork. V is a neck of sheet-iron four inches deep. The valve is closed with mercury to about one-third of its height. An enlarged section of the valve is shown at Y. The tube T and the siphon S reach nearly to the bottom of the carboy. The former admits air, and as none can pass out evaporation is prevented. The siphon is jointed with rubber at *a*, and has a stopcock at *b*. It is furnished at the lower end with a piece of rubber tubing for connecting with the lower part of the pipette P ; which is supported by brackets *c c*, affixed to the wall of the room or an upright standard. The upper extremity of the pipette P, passes through a vessel *d*, designed to catch the liquid running over. The method of using the apparatus is to attach the tube to the pipette, open the pinch-cock *e*, allow the normal solution to flow upwards into the pipette, until the latter overflows. Stop the flow, close with the finger, remove the rubber tube and wipe off any of the solution adhering to the outside of the pipette, which is now ready, on removing the finger, to deliver 100 c.c. of the normal solution. Fig. 30 shows a very convenient apparatus for holding the glass bottle which receives the liquid from the pipette and catching the drippings. *c* is a cylinder of tin-plate to receive the assay bottle. E is a sponge enveloped in linen, forced into a tube of tin-plate, terminated above by a cup and open below, so that the liquid may run into the vessel B, on which the tube is soldered. The whole apparatus is affixed to a sheet of tin-plate, movable in two slots R R. The extent of movement is determined by two stops t t, so placed that when the base of the apparatus abuts against one of them, the pipette will be in contact with the sponge. When it strikes the other it will be directly over the center of the neck of the bot

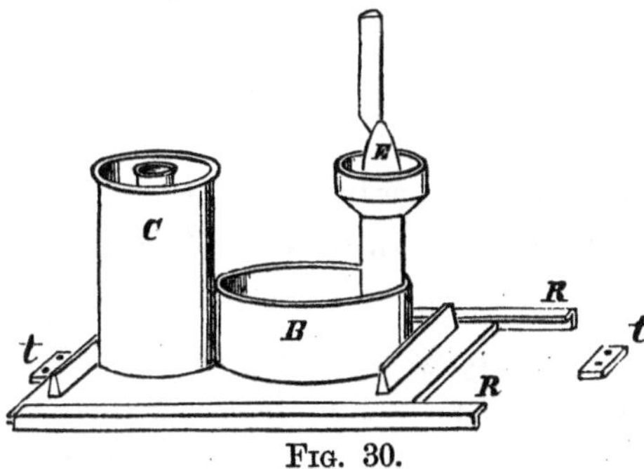

FIG. 30.

REMARKS.—The precipitated chloride of silver must be exposed to the light as little as possible. Sunlight converts the chloride into a sub-chloride, liberating chlorine, and this vitiates the results. The action of sunlight may be prevented by windows of yellow glass, which excludes chemical rays. If the bullion treated contains mercury, sunlight will not blacken the combined chlorides; the mercury may be held in solution by adding 10 gms. of acetate of soda containing a little free acetic acid. Test for the presence of mercury by standing the bottle in the light. The temperature of the normal solution should remain the same as that at which it was standardized. The most convenient temperature is 68° F., and the solution should be made and kept in a separate room, the heat of which can be regulated by a good thermometer.

Despite all precautions the normal solution will become stronger in time through evaporation of water. This will demand correction, and in regular practice it is customary to take a certain weight of pure silver and subject it to the same operation as the regular assays. The latter are corrected according to the indications of the proof assay. 1.005 grammes of silver is a convenient weight to take.

The strength of the concentrated salt solution can also be determined by finding how many c.c. will be required to precipitate one gm. of pure silver; the concentrated salt solution being run from a graduated pipette a few drops at a time. If we have determined by evaporation the salt in one c.c., we simply divide .54167 by the weight found, and we have the number of c.c. of concentrated solution to be diluted to 100.

The presence of sulphide of silver or antimony, and tin sometimes interferes in making the silver bullion assay. The first two may be removed by boiling with stronger acid. For the latter a little nitre and sulphuric acid will make a clear solution. (See Report of the Director of the U. S. Mint for 1875).

The pure silver required for standardizing and check assays may be made by dissolving tough bar silver in nitric acid, and precipitating with pure hydrochloric. The white precipitate being well washed, and fused with bi-carbonate of soda, and the button obtained re-melted with borax to purify it.

The chloride can also be reduced with zinc and dilute sulphuric acid, and the fine silver obtained melted down with borax glass; re-melting to purify.

GOLD BULLION.

The assay of gold coin and bullion comprises two determinations. *a*. Base metal. *b*. Gold. The difference between these two, and the total weight of bullion gives the amount of silver.

a. BASE METAL: CUPELLATION.—Weigh out 0.500 gms. and cupel with ten times its weight of pure lead rolled out into a sheet, the bullion being wrapped in it. If the bullion contain much copper, use more lead, or one-half the weight of bullion.

The copper is oxidized and carried into the cupel by the litharge, leaving a button of gold, and silver, if there be any.

A check assay is made with every set of assays. We employ for this a proof-alloy containing 850 parts of gold, 12 parts of copper, and the rest silver. This ought to lose by cupellation just 12 parts of copper. It may lose more or less, and according to the difference one way or other, we correct the regular assays which have been made under the same conditions. A fine gold proof is also made.

b. Gold, Parting.—Take for this operation 0.5 grammes of the alloy and add two and one-half times its weight of pure silver. Wrap the alloy and silver in a sheet of lead and cupel. If the alloy be over 950 fine, add, say 0.005 gms. of rolled copper to toughen the cornet. This addition should also be used in the fine gold proof. The button obtained from cupellation is hammered on the anvil to flatten. Three blows with a light hammer will suffice. It is then heated to redness in a clay annealing cup, and passed between the rolls of a small flattening mill. When rolled, the ribbon is again annealed and wound into a cornet or spiral.

The cornet is subjected to the action of nitric acid in a glass matrass of about three ounces capacity (Fig. 24). Acid of two different degrees of strength is employed. The first has a specific gravity of 1.16 (21° Beaumé); the second a gravity of 1.26 (32° Beaumé). If very strong acid were used at first the action would be too brisk and might break up the cornet. First pour on the acid of 1.16 specific gravity, and heat for ten minutes; replace this with acid of 1.26 specific gravity, and boil ten minutes; decant, and make a second boiling with acid of the same strength (1.26) for another ten minutes. A gentle boiling is intended, and not a tumbling about of the cornet. Finally the cornet is washed, the flask filled completely with distilled water, an annealing-cup placed over the neck, and the whole is inverted. The cornet falls into the cup, the flask is removed, the water decanted, and the cornet dried and annealed. The weight of this cornet gives the amount of gold in the sample assayed. The gold, copper, and silver are reported in thousandths.

REMARKS.—The government use for test assay of gold coins, an alloy of, gold 900, copper 75, and silver 25 parts.

Proof gold for test assays can be made by dissolving as pure metal as obtainable in aqua regia, diluting the solution largely and allowing it to stand, to settle any chloride of silver, the filtered solution being then concentrated to crystallization, diluted with pure water, and the gold precipitated with oxalic acid, filtered off, well washed, dried and fused with borax and nitre ; re-fusing to purify. Sulphate of iron may be used in place of oxalic acid for precipitation, but tests made in the Royal Mint, London, proves the former to be the best.

CHLORINATION ASSAY.

To determine the percentage of chlorination, weigh out two samples of the chloridized ore or "pulp," each $\frac{1}{10}$ A.T. Scorify one with 30 gms of lead, and cupel. Place the second sample in a filter paper and wash with a strong solution of hyposulphite of soda in water (two pounds to the gallon) until all the chloride of silver in the "pulp" has been dissolved. This can be determined by adding a drop of a solution of sulphide of sodium in water to a test sample of the filtrate. When no black precipitate or brown color is formed, the chloride of silver is all dissolved, and the desired point has been reached. Wash the residue with pure water, dry and burn the filter in a dish or scoop, in the cupel muffle.

Mix the ashes with 30 gms. of pure lead, scorify and cupel. The calculation can best be shown by example:

The "pulp" untreated gave 208 ozs. of silver per ton
The "pulp" treated " 14 " " " "

still remaining in the ore unchloridized. Hence, to determine the percentage of silver chloridized form the proportion: 208 : (208—14) :: 100 : x

In the West, nearly all silver reducing works make these assays every day, as the amount of chloridized silver is all that can be extracted by amalgamation.

Remarks.—This method is sufficiently accurate to check the chlorination of the ore, and with proper care, duplicate assays are unnecessary.

The operations of scorification and cupellation are conducted as already described under the head of silver ores.

The success of the process depends upon the care taken in washing

SCHEME FOR PLATINUM.

Treat one gm. of ore or alloy, with hydrochloric acid, filter and wash. This will separate the iron and soluble constituents. Treat the residue with nitric and muriatic acid, the latter being in excess, and digest for some time; eight to fifteen hours. The residue will consist of silica and most of the iridium and osmium. The solution will contain the platinum more or less pure according to the number of other metals contained in the ore. Evaporate it nearly to dryness and add twice its bulk of alcohol, and chloride of ammonium, until a precipitate ceases to form. Filter, wash, and dry; then transfer filter and contents to a clay crucible ; cover and heat gradually, and finally intensely, cool, and weigh the residue of platinum sponge. This method is of course approximate only, as it is difficult to separate all iridium, and other metals ; but for practical purposes it is sufficiently close.

To determine the constituents of the ore which are of no value, charge two gms. of ore, and ten gms. of granulated silver, well mixed, in a small crucible, the sides of which have been glazed with borax (melt some borax in it), over the mixture of borax and silver put ten gms. borax glass and one or two pieces of charcoal. Fuse and keep hot for for some time ; cool, break, and weigh the button of alloy ; after carefully removing the borax glass. Subtract the weight of the button from the sum of the weights of the ore and silver. The difference equals the impurities in the ore. The button can then be treated with nitric acid to dissolve the silver, by the method given above.

REMARKS.—When the proportion of silver in the button is very large, the nitric acid will dissolve the platinum also. The above methods have been tried with success on various platinum compounds. In sponging the platinum, it should be wrapped in paper first, and covered to prevent loss. Care must be taken to drive out all the ammonia salts, by raising the temperature toward the last.

SCHEME FOR ZINC.

The ore may contain lead, arsenic, antimony, sulphur, gold, silver, copper, zinc, manganese, iron, silica, alumina, lime, and magnesia. To determine the zinc. Weigh out one to four gms. of ore, according to its richness. Treat with ten c.c. nitric, five c.c. muriatic, and ten c.c. sulphuric acid, adding each separately and in order, increasing the quantity if necessary. All the acids should be concentrated. Evaporate nearly to dryness in a porcelain casserole; moisten with dilute muriatic acid, and dilute with water. Pass sulphuretted hydrogen gas through the solution as described on page 42. Warm, filter, and wash.

Residue A	Filtrate A
Will contain the lead, arsenic, antimony, sulphur, gold, silver, silica, and most of the lime.	Will contain the zinc, manganese, iron, alumina, and magnesia. Boil with one or two crystals of chlorate of potash, nearly neutralize with carbonate of soda, until a reddish color appears; boil and add acetate of soda (4 to 8 gms). Boil for ten to twenty minutes, filter and wash.
Residue B	**Filtrate B**
Will contain the iron and alumina.	Will contain the manganese, zinc, and magnesia.

Add acetic acid, and saturate with sulphuretted hydrogen gas, warm and filter. Wash carefully with sulphuretted hydrogen water once or twice.

Residue C	Filtrate C
Will contain zinc and sulphur	Manganese and magnesia.

Dissolve residue C on the filter with warm hydrochloric acid, add a little chlorate of potash to the solution, and boil. Add carbonate of soda until a precipitate ceases to form. Filter and wash the precipitate, dry on the paper and ignite in a platinum crucible. Weigh after cooling. Deduct the weight of the crucible and filter paper from the last weight and multiply the difference by .8026. The product will be the metallic zinc.

The percentage can be determined by the formula. Percent. of $\text{zinc} = \frac{\text{zinc} \times 100}{\text{weight of ore taken.}}$

If the ore contains no manganese, instead of precipitating filtrate *a* with acetate of soda, boil it with two or three crystals of chlorate of potash, and add ammonia in excess the residue will contain the iron and alumina, the filtrate the zinc, which can be determined volumetrically by the following method:

Prepare a solution of sulphide of sodium in water (100 gms. to 1000 or 1200 c.c. of water), and standardize with a solution of zinc made by dissolving 10 gms. pure zinc in hydrochloric acid and diluting to 1 litre. The operation is performed by measuring off 50 c.c. of zinc solution in a beaker, adding ammonia until the precipitate is re-dissolved, then 400 c.c. of water; afterward running in the sulphide of sodium solution from a pipette until a drop of the zinc solution tested with chloride of nickel on a porcelain plate turns blackish gray. Note the number of c.c. of sulphide of sodium used, and repeat to be certain. Knowing the amount of zinc in the solution, the value of the sulphide of sodium solution per c.c. is very easily calculated. This done, the ammonia solution of zinc from filtrate *a* can be divided and tested in the same manner.

Calculation. The number of c.c. of sodium solution employed multiplied by the value per c.c. gives the amount of zinc=Z. $\frac{Z \times 100}{\text{Weight of ore taken}}$=the per cent.

REMARKS.—An ore containing sulphide of zinc was treated by the first method, the assays being made in duplicate:

No. 1 gave.................... 2.380 per cent. metallic zinc.
" 2 " .... 2.367 " " "

DETERMINATION OF BISMUTH IN AN ALLOY.

Weigh out two gms. of the alloy, and treat with concentrated nitric acid until action ceases. Evaporate to dryness, add 50 to 100 drops of strong sulphuric acid. Mix with a glass rod, and evaporate to dryness. Add water with a few drops of sulphuric acid and boil. Filter, and to the solution add an excess of carbonate of ammonia. Collect the precipitated, oxide of bismuth on a filter, wash, and dry. Separate carefully from the filter, ignite in a porcelain crucible and weigh. Every 100 parts of the weight found corresponds to 89.87 of metallic bismuth. (See Mitchell, p. 642.)

Remarks.—The bismuth may also be precipitated from the prepared solution by either lead, or copper; and after washing and drying, be weighed in a metallic form, or redissolved and precipitated as above. In this case copper will be the best preciptant.

DETERMINATION OF TIN IN THE WET WAY.

The various methods that have been employed for the determination of tin in the wet way may be classed under two heads:

a. The substance is an ore. This may consist of an oxide or sulphide of tin, and be associated with iron, copper, zinc, bismuth, arsenic, antimony, manganese, silica, lime, magnesia, and alumina; occasionally molybdenum, tungstic, tantalic or niobic acids.

b. The substance is an alloy, which may contain iron, copper, zinc, bismuth, arsenic, antimony, tungsten, and molybdenum.

a. Treatment of ores. Pulverize finely.

1. If the ore contain volatile ingredients roast as in the dry assay, and treat the residue with nitro-hydrochloric acid

(conc.), (3 parts of hydrochloric to 1 of nitric), to dissolve iron, copper, etc. Boil nearly to dryness, cool, dilute with water and digest. Filter. The residue will contain the oxide of tin and silica, possibly the tungstic acid, etc. Wash, and if tungstic acid is suspected, digest with caustic ammonia for about one hour. Filter, wash, dry, and treat the residue by fire assay, or by one of the methods given below. Instead of treating the roasted ore with acids, it may be fused with bi-sulphate of potash in excess, which decomposes the silicates in the ore, and dissolves the bases; the fused mass treated with water and hydrochloric acid, the residue filtered off, washed, dried, and treated by dry assay or wet, as the case may be. The addition of cryolite or fluoride of potassium in the fusion with bi-sulphate of potassium gives good results.

2. Determination of tin in the purified ore.

Method by fusion with sulphur. Weigh out one gm. and mix with five gms. of powdered sulphur, and five gms. of dry carbonate of soda. Place the mixture in a porcelain crucible, cover and heat over a Bunsen burner, or alcohol lamp, until liquid. Keep fused for ten or fifteen minutes; cool and treat the fused mass with water, filter and wash. Test the residue for tin with the blowpipe, and if any be present re-fuse, and add the solution to the one obtained in the first fusion.

Place the solutions in a large beaker, and treat with dilute sulphuric or hydrochloric acid until a precipitate ceases to form; boil, filter by decantation, and wash with sulphuretted hydrogen water. Dry the residue and ignite in a weighed porcelain crucible, to expel sulphur, adding a few drops of nitric acid to oxidize toward the last. Weigh until constant. The addition of a little carbonate of am monia in the ignition will help to expel any sulphuric acid. The ignited residue consists of binoxide of tin and silica; if great accuracy is required, it should be purified either by heating with fluoride of ammonium until the weight is constant, or reducing the binoxide of tin with hydrogen, dissolving the metal produced in hydrochloric acid, washing and weighing the residue. The loss represents the binoxide of tin. The weight of binoxide found, multiplied by $\frac{59}{75}$, gives the metallic tin.

Street gas may be used instead of hydrogen, the weighed precipitate being placed in the bulb of a small chloride of calcium tube, through which the gas is passed, the bulb being heated.

Method by fusion with caustic potash:

Weigh out one gramme and fuse with six to ten gms. of caustic potash in a silver crucible. The potash being placed in the crucible with its own weight of water, the ore stirred in, and the whole mass evaporated to dryness, and then heated for one half hour, until fusion is complete. Dissolve the fused mass in water and hydrochloric acid, and boil; any tin ore unacted upon filter off and re-fuse. Evaporate to dryness, moisten with hydrochloric acid and water, digest, filter and wash. The solution will contain the tin free from silica, tungstic acid, etc.

The tin can be precipitated from the solution with zinc, in the metallic state, collected, washed and weighed, or it may be precipitated with sulphuretted hydrogen and the precipitate filtered off, washed, ignited, and weighed as binoxide.

In cases where the ore has been purified with acids, or by fusion with bisulphate of potash, the silica may be expelled until the weight is constant with fluoride of ammonium, and the residue weighed as binoxide. The results are, however, liable to be too high.

b. The substance is an alloy.

1. Dissolve in hot hydrochloric acid, filter, and wash. Precipitate the filtrate with zinc. Collect the precipitated metals, dry, and ignite; treat with concentrated nitric acid and wash. Dry the residue, and weigh as binoxide.

2. Oxidize the finely divided alloy (filings) with nitric acid, sp. gr. 1.3. Add water, digest and filter, wash, ignite, and weigh the residue as binoxide of tin.

REMARKS.—Slags which contain stannates. Pulverize, and afterwards digest with water, filter, and treat the solution with dilute sulphuric acid.

The best way is to neutralize the solution with ammonia, add a little hydrochloric acid to dissolve any precipitate formed, then the sulphuric acid, and dilute. Allow to stand for several hours before filtering off the precipitate formed. Ignite and weigh as binoxide. Watts' Dictionary of Chemistry, Vol. 5, page 811.

Comparison of results obtained by various methods in the assay laboratory.

ORE.	METHOD BY FUSION WITH SULPHUR.	METHOD BY FLUORIDE.	METHOD WITH HYDROGEN.
Durango,	76.8	76.8	——
"	76.3	76.4	——
"	76.2	76.4	——
Locality unknown,	74.8	75.5	75.0
" "	74.7	75.7	——

SCHEME FOR COPPER.

Roast five gms. of the finely powdered ore with the addition of a little charcoal, and carbonate of ammonia toward the last. Treat the residue, in a covered casserole, with five c.c. hydrochloric, ten c.c. nitric, and ten c.c. sulphuric acid, concentrated, and added in order. Evaporate until heavy white fumes come off in excess. Cool, dilute with a little water and digest, filter, and wash the residue until the filtrate does not turn black with sulphuretted hydrogen solution. Test the residue with the blowpipe for copper.

The solution will contain the copper as sulphate, and can be treated in several ways. The best are,

a. Precipitation by the battery.

b. Precipitation by zinc or iron.

c. Volumetric determination.

Divide the solution in five equal parts by volume.

a. Precipitation by the battery.

Place the acid solution of copper in a weighed platinum dish; set the dish upon a spiral of copper wire connecting the zinc element of a Bunsen cell, and have in the solution a piece of clean platinum foil, suspended from another wire connecting with the carbon element. Test for the complete precipitation of the copper by taking out a little of the solution and adding sulphuretted hydrogen; if no color is observed, the precipitation is complete. Decant the fluid from the red precipitate of copper, wash once with water, and twice with alcohol. Dry by burning out the alcohol, and weigh. This weight, less the weight of the dish, equals metallic copper. The operation of drying and weighing must be conducted as quickly as possible.

b. Precipitation by zinc or iron.

Pour one part of the solution of copper in a porcelain dish, in which is placed a weighed slip of platinum foil. Rest upon the latter a piece of pure zinc (Lehigh zinc will do), and add dilute sulphuric acid until fumes cease to come off, and the zinc is dissolved. The solution should then be clear and give no color with sulphuretted hydrogen. Pour off the liquid, press the copper together, and wash with water and alcohol; dry, and weigh the copper and foil. This weight, less that of the foil, gives the copper.

The precipitation by iron is conducted in much the same manner, save that the solution should be nearly neutral, and no platinum foil is required. The iron used should be clean and pure; it may be either sheet or wire.

c. Volumetric determination.

Take one part of the prepared solution of copper, and add ammonia in excess until the precipitate formed is dissolved; the solution should be a deep blue. Then titrate with a prepared solution of cyanide of potassium until the blue color disappears. The number of c.c. of cyanide used indicates the amount of copper present. The cyanide solution is made by dissolving sixty to seventy gms. commercial cyanide of potassium in two quarts of water, and standardizing it with a solution of pure copper, of known value. This is made by dissolving five gms of pure copper in nitric acid, boiling and diluting to one litre. A portion of this solution can then be treated with cyanide, and the value of the latter in copper per c.c. ascertained. Should zinc, nickel, cobalt, or manganese be present in the ore treated, it is well to precipitate the copper with zinc in a porcelain dish, wash with water, and re-dissolve in nitric acid. Then add ammonia and proceed wilh the tetration. The solution of cyanide should be kept in a green bottle, tightly stoppered, and away from the light.

REMARKS.—Determinations of copper in a mixture of iron and copper pyrites gave, by precipitation with sheet iron, 16.6 per cent.; by volumetric estimation with cyanide solution 16.53 and 16.35 per cent. Another sample gave 8.4 and 8.6 per cent., and a third specimen gave: by battery, 1.3 per cent., with zinc, 1.3 per cent.

SCHEME FOR IRON.

Volumetric. Weigh out 1 gm. of the finely powdered ore. Fuse in a platinum or porcelain crucible, with 4 to 6 gms. carbonate of soda and ½ to 1 gm. of nitrate of soda, well mixed; until the whole mass is in quiet fusion. Then cool and dissolve in a casserole with water, acidulating gradually with hydrochloric acid, until gas ceases to come off. Keep covered to prevent loss. Heat for some time, filter and wash.

Treat the filtrate with ammonia until a precipitate ceases to form; boil, filter, and wash once or twice, and then dissolve the precipitate in dilute sulphuric acid on the filter, and wash. The solution containing the iron as sulphate is placed in a 6 oz. bottle with a clean strip of platinum foil and a small piece of amalgamated zinc free from iron. Allow it to stand several hours, then transfer to a large beaker and titrate with a standard solution of permanganate of potash prepared as follows: Make a solution of crystalline permanganate of potash in water and standardize it with a solution of pure sulphate of iron of known value.

The latter is prepared by dissolving .2 gms. of fine iron piano-forte wire, well cleaned, in a four ounce flask with dilute sulphuric acid. The flask should be closed so that the gas evolved can pass out and no air enter. To effect this, stop the flask with a cork in which is fitted a glass tube about two inches long, on the end of which is a piece of rubber tubing closed at the extremity with a small piece of glass rod and slit on one side. In this way a valve is formed which allows the gas to escape. Heat just enough to dissolve the wire, and when this is effected decant into a medium sized beaker, wash the flask out, adding the wash water to the solution in the beaker (use cold water); then add 5. to 10 c.c. dilute sulphuric acid, and titrate with the permanganate solution, adding it a c.c. at a time from a graduated burette.

The weight of the iron taken, multiplied by .997, = the weight of pure metallic iron to which the cubic centimeters of permanganate used is equivalent. All that is necessary is to find the value of 1 c.c. of permanganate, and in testing an ore multiply it by the number of c.c. used. The product equals the metallic iron in the ore.

The presence of titanium interferes with this method.

In this case the solution in the reduction bottle will have a pink tinge after standing. To separate the iron and titanic acid, dry, and ignite the ammonia precipitate in a glass tube which can be heated strongly over a burner, hydrogen (street gas) being passed through the tube; dissolve the iron and proceed as above. The same precautions should be observed in keeping the permanganate solution as in the case of the cyanide, given in the scheme for copper.

REMARKS—A sample of magnetite and hematite gave by this method, duplicate assays being made,

No. 1 .... 52.304 per cent. iron.
No. 2 .... 52.416 " "

The ore contained no titanic acid.

SCHEME FOR MANGANESE.

Manganese occurs in an oxidized form, and its principal ores are

Pyrolusite (black oxide) (MnO_2)............=18 per cent.
Braunite (sesquioxide) (Mn_2O_3)..............=10 "
Manganite (gray manganese ore)($Mn_2 O_3+H_2O$)= 9 "
Psilomelane (hydrate) ($Mn_2O_3+H_2O$).........= 9 "
Hausmanite (red manganese oxide) (Mn_3O_4)..=6.8 "

The quantity of oxygen which an ore of manganese is capable of yielding generally regulates its commercial value; hence, it is only necessary to determine the amount of binoxide contained, which can be arrived at very easily by the following method; sufficiently accurate for practical purposes.

Assay.—Weigh out 1 to 2 gms. of the finely pulverized ore, place in a small flask, and add from 5 to 7 gms. of neutral oxalate of potash in powder, and a little water. Close the flask with a plug of cotton and weigh. Then add about 30 c.c. of sulphuric acid, a little at a time. The sulphuric acid should be weighed in a small flask, which should be again weighed when empty, to determine the actual weight of sulphuric acid added to the ore. When effervescence has ceased, heat the flask containing the ore gently until every trace of black powder in the same has disappeared. Cool and weigh. The amount of peroxide of manganese can be estimated from the carbonic acid driven off, as follows: Deduct the weight of the flask and residue from the sum of the first weight, and the sulphuric acid used, and multiply the difference by 0.9887 the product will be the amount of binoxide of manganese contained in the ore taken.

REMARKS.—When the ores contain carbonates (which can be ascertained by testing with nitric acid), after weighing out the ore, treat it with a solution of one part of sulphuric acid to five parts of water, until the carbonates are decomposed. Wash, and then add the weighed oxalate of potash and more acid.

The process given above, in order to be perfectly accurate, should be performed in an air-tight apparatus with the greatest care, so that nothing but carbonic acid can escape, and no moist air enter; but for practical purposes, the apparatus given will do.

A sample of manganese ore treated by this method gave 64 per cent. of binoxide. The same sample gave 63.9 per cent. of binoxide by determining the metallic manganese, and calculating the amount of oxide it would form. For this test, however, the apparatus was nearly air-tight, and a little more perfect than the one described above; but on the same principle.

DETERMINATION OF NICKEL.

Weigh out one or two gms. of ore and roast carefully, adding charcoal, and carbonate of ammonia toward the end of the operation. Treat the roasted ore with hydrochloric, nitric, and sulphuric acids, as in the method for copper. Cool, and add water and sulphuric acid. Pass sulphuretted hydrogen through the solution; warm, filter, and wash. Boil the filtrate to expel excess of sulphuretted hydrogen, and to convert the iron present into a sesqui-salt. Treat with ammonia in excess; boil, filter, and wash. The solution will contain the nickel as a sulphate. Allow it to stand three or four hours, and filter off any precipitate formed;

then place the solution in a platinum dish, and treat as in the determination of copper, keeping the solution ammoniacal instead of acid.

REMARKS.—This method tried on poor nickel ore gave excellent results. 0.12 per cent. being the lowest amount determined.

SCHEME FOR SULPHUR.

SOURCES.—Native sulphur, and sulphides of the metals, more or less pure. The sulphide of iron (pyrite) (FeS_2), being most used.

ASSAY.—This is made by distillation, and in the wet way, The latter is the best.

To conduct the first, weigh out a portion of the finely pulverized ore, and heat it in a retort; which should be furnished with a receiver to collect the sublimed sulphur. The retort may be of glass if the ore is sulphurous earth, but must be of iron if pyrites; the latter should also be mixed with sand, to prevent its fusing together. The heat for pyrites should be full red.

The product of distillation is weighed and should be examined by the wet way to determine its purity; hence it is generally better to test the ore in this way at once. Weigh out one to two gms. of the finely pulverized ore and oxidize with nitric acid and chlorate of potash, in a flask, until action ceases; then filter and wash. If the residue contains sulphur, dry and weigh it; then ignite and weigh. The difference will be the sulphur unoxidized; add to this a little hydrochloric acid, and then chloride of barium in slight excess, heat for a few moments, and allow the particles to settle. Pour off the liquid through a filter, and wash with dilute hydrochloric acid, then with water. Dry and ignite the residue in a porcelain crucible. Multiply the weight of the precipitate less that of the filter ash by $\frac{16}{116.5}$; the product equals the sulphur in the sample taken.

REMARKS.—A sample tested by the latter method gave 32.52 per cent. and 32.55 per cent. of sulphur; two separate weighings being made for the analysis, and the precipitates tested to determine their purity.

PART IV.

TABLES AND REFERENCES.

PRECIOUS STONES.

ARRANGED ACCORDING TO HARDNESS.

NAME.	COLOR.	HARDNESS.	SPECIFIC GRAVITY.	ACTION OF ACIDS.	BLOWPIPE CHARACTERISTICS.
Diamond.	Colorless, smokey, yellow, green, blue, and black.	10.	3.55	Not acted on.	Burns at an intense heat, without residue.
Sapphire (Corundum).	Colorless, blue, red, yellow, gray, and brown.	9.	3.9 to 4	Insoluble.	Infusible.
Topaz.	Colorless, yellow, blue, greenish-blue.	8.	3.5	Not acted on.	Infusible, cracks at a high heat.
Ruby (Spinel).	Red, blue, green, yellow, white, and black.	8.	3.5 to 4.9	Insoluble in hydrochloric acid. Partly soluble in sulphuric acid.	Infusible, changes color.
Emerald (Aquamarine, Beryl).	Green, blue, yellow, red, and white.	7.5 to 8	2.6 to 2.7	Not acted on.	Fuses with difficulty on the edges.
Zircon.	Colorless, yellow, red, brown, pink, and green.	7.5	4. to 4.7	Insoluble.	Infusible.
Agate, Jasper, Amethyst, Onyx, etc (Quartz).	Colorless, white, black, red, and green.	7.	2.5 to 2.7	Insoluble.	Infusible, except with carbonate of soda.
Garnet.	Red, brown, yellow, white, green, and black.	7. to 6.5	3.15 to 4	Imperfectly soluble.	Fusible.
Turquoise.	Blue, white, yellow, and red.	6.	2.6 to 2.8	Soluble.	Infusible.
Lapis-Lazuli.	Blue, red, green, and colorless.	5.5 to 5	2.3 to 2.4	Gelatinizes.	Fuses with intumescence and gives a blue bead.
Opal.	Brown, green, and gray.	6.5 to 5.5	1.9 to 2.3	More or less soluble.	Infusible, gives off water and becomes opaque.
Malachite.	Bright green.	4 to 3.5	3.7 to 4	Soluble with effervescence.	Gives off water and Fuses.

SCALE OF HARDNESS.

1. Easily scratched with the nail.

2. Not easily scratched with the nail. Does not scratch a copper coin.

3. Scratches and is scratched by a copper coin.

4. Not scratched by a copper coin; does not scratch glass.

5. Scratches glass with difficulty; easily scratched with the knife.

6. Scratches glass easily. Not easily scratched by the knife.

7. Not scratched by the knife; yields with difficulty to the file.

8. Harder than flint.

9. Harder still.

10. Diamond.

METALS—CHARACTERISTICS.

INCLUDING CARBON AND SULPHUR.

METAL.	COLOR.	HARDNESS.	SPECIFIC GRAVITY.	BEST SOLVENTS.	ON CHARCOAL, BEFORE THE BLP.	FUSIBILITY. FAHRENHEIT.
Lead.	Bluish, malleable.	1.5	11.45	Nitric or Muriatic.	Fuses and gives a yellow coat.	234°
Antimony.	Bluish-white, brittle.	3—3.5	6.8	Aqua regia	Fuses and gives off white fumes.	425°
Silver.	White, malleable.	2.5—3	10.5—11.1	Nitric and sulphuric.	Fuse , gives reddish coat with long blowing.	916°—1040°
Gold	Yellow, malleable.	2.5—3	15—19	Aqua regia	Fuses to a button.	2016°
Platinum.	Whitish to steel-gray, malleable.	4—4.5	16—19	Aqua regia	Infusible.	In flame of oxy. h. Blp.
Zinc.	Bluish-white, malleable, brittle.	2.	6.8—7,2	All acids.	Oxydizes and gives a white coat.	412°
Mercury.	Tin-white, liquid.	1—	13.5	Nitric.	Volatilizes.	Solid at-40.5°
Bismuth.	Reddish to silver white, brittle.	2—3.5	9.7	Nitric.	Fuses and gives an orange yellow coat.	268.3°
Tin.	Like silver, more bluish, malleable.	4—5	7.28	Muriatic. Sulphuric.	Gives metallic globule and white coat.	235°
Copper.	Red, malleable.	2.5—3	8.9	Conc. acids.	Can be fused to a bead.	1090°

METALS.	COLOR.	HARDNESS.	SPECIFIC GRAVITY.	BEST SOLVENTS,	ON CHARCOAL, BEFORE THE BLP.	FUSIBILITY, FAHRENHEIT.
Iron.	Gray, malleable, magnetic.	4—5	7.3—7.8	All acids.	Infusible.	Highest heat of Forge 1.500—1.600
Manganese.	Grayish-white, brittle.	9—10	7.1—8.01	Nitric, sulphuric, muriatic.	Infusible.	"
Nickel.	Silver-white, malleable, magnetic.	5—6	8.2—8.7	Nitric.	Infusible,	"
Cobalt.	Steel-gray to red, magnetic.	5—6	8.5—8.7	Nitric.	Infusible.	"
Carbon.	Colorless to Black.	Variable.	Variable.	Insoluble.	Infusible—burns.	Infusible.
Sulphur.	Yellow, reddish, greenish, brittle.	1—2.5	2.07	Oil of Turpentine, etc.	Melts and gives off sulphurous acid.	111°—114°

The value of the various metals changes according to the production and demand, save in the case of gold which has a standard value of twenty dollars and sixty-seven cents per Troy ounce in gold coin, when perfectly pure; the price being determined as follows:

By the laws of the United States the composition of the gold coins for every one hundred parts, by weight, is 90 parts of pure gold and 10 parts of alloy.

Eight hundred dollars in U. S. gold coin weighs 43 ounces Troy, $\frac{9}{10}$ of this weight must, therefore, be pure gold= 38.7 ounces. $\frac{800}{38.7} = 20.6718$ dollars; this then is the coin value of one ounce.

Before the immense production of silver depreciated the cost of that metal, a similar calculation gave its value in gold coin per Troy ounce. No comparison, however, can now be made, the price of silver being variable. The value was deduced as follows:

\$11.83 silver coin=11 ounces Troy, $\frac{9}{10}$ of this gives the pure metal=9.9. ounces. $\frac{12.80}{9.9}=1.2929$ as the coin value of pure silver.

ORES—CHARACTERISTICS.

LEAD.

ORES.	COMPOSITION.	COLOR.	HARDNESS.	SPECIFIC GRAVITY.	SOLUBILITY. SOLVENTS.	ON CHARCOAL, BEFORE THE BLOWPIPE.
Galena.	PbS.	Steel gray.	2.5—2.7	7.2—7.7	Nitric acid.	Gives off SO_2 and fuses.
Cerussite.	$PbCO_3$	Variable.	3—3.5	6.4	Muriat c with effervescence.	Cracks and fuses.
Anglesite.	PbSO4	White, tinged with yellow, etc.	2.7—3	6.2	Insoluble.	"
Pyromorphite.	$3Pb.3P_2O_5+PbCl_2$.	Green, yellow, brown, blue.	3.5—4	6.5—7	Soluble.	Fusible, lead coat.

ANTIMONY.

ORES.	COMPOSITION.	COLOR.	HARDNESS.	SPECIFIC GRAVITY.	SOLUBILITY. SOLVENTS.	ON CHARCOAL, BEFORE THE BLOWPIPE.
Stibnite.	Sb_2S_3.	Lead-gray to blackish.	2	4.5—4.6	Soluble.	Fuses easily and gives off white fumes.
Oxides.	Sb_2O_3. Sb_2O_5.	Variable.	2—3	5—5.5	Muriatic and aqua regia.	Fuses and volatilizes

SILVER.

ORES.	COMPOSITION.	COLOR.	HARDNESS.	SPECIFIC GRAVITY.	SOLUBILITY. SOLVENTS.	ON CHARCOAL, BEFORE THE BLOWPIPE.
Native silver and alloys. Compounds with S.As.Sb. Cl.Br.I.Te.Se etc.	See page 133.	Variable.	Variable.	Variable.	Nitric acid and aqua regia.	Gives, when fused on charcoal with soda and test lead, and the button cupelled; a bead of silver.

GOLD.

ORES.	COMPOSITION.	COLOR.	HARDNESS.	SPECIFIC GRAVITY.	SOLUBILITY. SOLVENTS.	ON CHARCOAL, BEFORE THE BLOWPIPE.
Native and alloys. Compounds with Te. and Se.	See page 134.	Generally yellow.	2.5—3	15—19	Aqua regia.	Fusible to a bead, better with borax glass.

PLATINUM.

ORES.	COMPOSITION.	COLOR.	HARDNESS.	SPECIFIC GRAVITY.	SOLUBILITY. SOLVENTS.	ON CHARCOAL, BEFORE THE BLOWPIPE.
Native and alloys.	Pb.Ir.As.Pd. etc.	Whiteish, blue and gray.	4—4.5	16—19	Aqua regia.	Infusible.

ZINC.

ORES.	COMPOSITION.	COLOR.	HARDNESS.	SPECIFIC GRAVITY.	SOLUBILITY. SOLVENTS.	ON CHARCOAL, BEFORE THE BLOWPIPE.
Blende.	ZnS.	Variable.	3.5—4	3.9—4	Nitric, and gives off H_2S	Infusible. Reaction for zinc.
Smithsonite.	$ZnCO_3$.	Variable.	5	4—4.4	Nitric and other acids. Effervesces.	Infusible. Reaction for zinc.
Calamine.	$Zn_2 SiO_3$	Variable.	5	3.3—3.5	Glatinizes.	Fuses with difficulty. Reaction for zinc
Zincite.	ZnO.	Red.	4—4.5	5.4—5.8	All acids.	Infusible. Reaction for zinc.

MERCURY.

ORES.	COMPOSITION.	COLOR.	HARDNESS.	SPECIFIC GRAVITY.	SOLUBILITY. SOLVENTS.	ON CHARCOAL, BEFORE THE BLOWPIPE.
Mercury.	Hg.	Tin-white.	—1	13.5	Nitric acid.	Volatile.
Cinnabar.	HgS.	Red.	2—2.5	8.9	Aqua regia.	Volatile, gives fumes SO_2
Calomel.	Hg_2Cl_2.	White to brown.	1—2	6.4	Aqua regia.	Volatile. White coat.

BISMUTH.

ORES.	COMPOSITION.	COLOR.	HARDNESS.	SPECIFIC GRAVITY.	SOLUBILITY. SOLVENTS.	ON CHARCOAL, BEFORE THE BLOWPIPE.
Native, Oxide, Sulphide, Arsenide.	Bi-S-As. Sometimes with Cu. Pb, etc.	Reddish to white. Variable when combined.	When pure metal. 2—2.5	When pure metal. 9.7	Nitric and muriatic.	Easily fusible. Volatile, giving yellow coat.

TIN.

ORES.	COMPOSITION.	COLOR.	HARDNESS.	SPECIFIC GRAVITY.	SOLUBILITY. SOLVENTS.	ON CHARCOAL, BEFORE THE BLOWPIPE.
Cassiterite.	SnO_2	Variable.	6—7	6.3—7.1	Insoluble.	Infusible. Reaction for tin.
Stanite.	Cu_2S } FeS } SnS_2	Steel gray to black.	4	4.3—4.5	Aqua regia.	Gives fumes of sulphurous acid and fuses

COPPER.

ORES.	COMPOSITION.	COLOR.	HARDNESS.	SPECIFIC GRAVITY.	SOLUBILITY. SOLVENTS.	ON CHARCOAL, BEFORE THE BLOWPIPE.
Native and alloys, oxidized ores and compounds, with S.As.Sb., etc.	See page 83.	Variable.	2—4.5	Native, 8.9 ores, 4—6	Nitric acid.	Fusible or reducible to metal, reaction for copper

IRON.

ORES.	COMPOSITION.	COLOR.	HARDNESS.	SPECIFIC GRAVITY.	SOLUBILITY. SOLVENTS.	ON CHARCOAL, BEFORE THE BLOWPIPE.
Magnetite.	Fe_3O_4	Black, magnetic.	5.5—6	4.9—5.1	Muriatic and aqua regia.	Fuses with difficulty.
Hematite.	Fe_2O_3	Red to black	5—6.5	4.5—5.3	Muriatic and aqua regia.	Infusible, becomes magnetic.
Limonite.	$2Fe_2O_33H_2O$	Dark brown	5—6.5	3.6—4	Muriatic warm.	Infusible, becomes magnetic.
Siderite.	$FeCO_3$	Variable.	3.5—4.5	3.7—3.9	Soluble with effervescence in hot acids.	Infusible, becomes magnetic.
Ilmenite.	$FeTiO_3$+ nFe_2O_3	Iron-black, slightly magnetic.	5—6	4.5—5	Aqua regia.	Infusible.
Franklinite.	3(FeO.ZnO. MnO).(Fe_2O_3 Mn_2O_3)	Black	5	5.5—6.5	Warm muriatic.	Infusible, reaction for zinc
Pyrite.	FeS_2	Yellow.	6—6.5	4.8—5	Nitric acid.	Gives off SO_2 and becomes magnetic. Fuses.

MANGANESE.

Oxidized ores	See page 120.	Dark brown to black.	1—6	3—5	Conc. muriatic; gives off Cl.	Infusible. Reaction for manganese.

NICKEL.

Nicolite.	Ni_2As.	Copper-red.	5—5.5	7.3—7.6	Aqua regia. Green solution.	Fuses with odor of As. Reaction for Ni.
Millerite.	NiS.	Brass or bronze-yellow.	3—3.5	5.2—5.6	Aqua regia.	Fuses to a brittle magnetic globule. Reaction for Ni.

COBALT.

Smaltite.	$CoAs_2$.	Tin-white to gray.	5.5—6	6.4—7	Nitric acid. Pink sol.	Gives off As, melts, and reaction for Co.
Cobaltite.	$(Co.Fe.Ni)As_2$	Silver-whiie to gray.	5.5	6—6.3	Nitric acid.	Gives off As, and becomes magnetic.

CARBON.

Diamond, Graphite, Coals, Lignite and Wood.	Pure to variable.	Colorless to black.	Variable.	Variable.	Insoluble.	Burns leaving an ash, save in the case of the diamond.

SULPHUR.

Sulphur and Sulphides.	Variable.	Yellow when pure.	Variable.	Variable.	When pure in bi-sulphide of carbon.	Melts and burns, giving off SO_2 in most cases.

SILVER.—ORES AND MINERALS.

MINERAL.	COMPOSITION.	PER CENT. OF SILVER. WHEN PURE.
1. Naumannite	AgSe	73.2
2. Eucairite	CuSe+AgSe	43.1
3. Hessite	AgTe	62.8
4. Sylvanite	$(AuAg)Te_3$	10—15
5. Silver Glance	AgS	87.04
6. Stromeyerite	(Ag,2Cu)S	2.96—53.1
7. Sternbergite	$AgS+3Fes+FeS_2$	34.2
8. Miargyrite	AgS,Sb_2S_3	36.7
9. Pyrargyrite	$3AgS,Sb_2S_3$	59.8
10. Proustite	$3AgS,As_2S_3$	65.4
11. Stephanite	$5AgS,Sb_2S_3$	68.5
12. Brogniardite	PbS,AgS,Sb_2S_3	26.1
13. Polybasite	$9(Ag,2Cu)S,(Sb,As)_2S_3$	68
14. Tetrahedrite	$4(2Cu, Fe, Zn, Ag, Hg)S, (Sb, As,Bi)_2S_3$	3.09—31.29
15. Xanthoconite	$(3AgS,As_2S_5)+2(3AgS,As_2S_3)$	64
16. Fireblende	Ag—Sb—S	62.3
17. Freieslebenite	$5(Pb,Ag)S,2Sb_2S_3$	22.24
18. Kerargyrite	AgCl	75.33
19. Bromyrite	AgBr	57.4
20. Embolite	Ag(Cl,Br)	61—71
21. Iodorite	AgI	46

Minerals often containing silver in small quantities:

1. Galena .... PbS.
2. Blende .... ZnS.
3. Pyrites .... FeS_2.
4. Chalcopyrite .... Cu_2S,Fe_2S_3.
5. Erubescite .... $3Cu_2S,Fe_2S_3$.
6. Mispickel .... FeS_2+FeAs_2

7. Altaite................PbTe.
8. Nagyagite............$(Pb,Au,Ag)_2(Te,Sb,S)_3$
9. Chiviatite.............$(Cu_2Pb)S.1\frac{1}{2}Bi_2S_3$.
10. Dufrenoysite..........$2PbS,As_2S_3$.
11. Enargite..............$3Cu_2S,As_2S_5$.
12. Slags, etc.
13. Cupel Bottoms, Dross, Litharge, etc.

SILVER—ALLOYS.

	Alloy.	Composition.	Per Ct. Silver, when pure.
1.	Native Silver	AgAu (generally)	
2.	Native Gold	AuAg	1—35
3.	Native Copper	CuAg	sometimes 10
4.	Chilenite	Ag_6Bi	86.2
5.	Bismuth Silver	Ag—Cu—As—Bi	60
6.	Discrasite, Antimonial Silver	Ag_2Sb	78
7.	Amalgam	$AgHg_2$	35
	"	$AgHg_3$	26
8.	Arquerite	Ag_6Hg	86.5
9.	Artificial Alloys, Silver Coin, Jewelry, etc.		

GOLD—MINERALS.

Sylvanite—Graphic Tellurium $(AuAg)Te_3$—Au 30—Ag 10.
Nagyagite—Foliated Tellurium $(Pb,Au,Ag)_2,Te,Sb,S)_3$—
Au 9—Ag 0.5.

GOLD—ALLOYS.

Native Gold................AuAg—Au 65—99.
Palladium Gold..Porpezite..AuPd—Au 85.98—Ag 4.17.
Rhodium Gold.............AuRd—Au 59—66.
Gold Amalgam.............$(AuAg)_2Hg_5$—Au 38.39—Ag 5.
Artificial Alloys, Gold Coin, Jewelry, etc.

COINS OF THE UNITED STATES.

(By Act of Congress, February 12, 1873.)

GOLD COINS.

DENOMINATION.	WEIGHT.	FINENESS.
Dollar, unit of value	25.8 grains.	900.
Quarter Eagle, $2.50	64.5 "	"
Three dollars	67.4 "	"
Half Eagle, $5	129.0 "	"
Eagle, $10	258.0 "	"
Double Eagle, $20	516.0 "	"

SILVER COINS.

DENOMINATION.	WEIGHT.	FINENESS.
Trade Dollar,	420 grains.	900.
Half Dollar, 50c.	12.5 grammes.	"
Quarter " 25c.	6.25 "	"
Dime, 10c.	2.5 "	"

MINOR COINS.

DENOMINATION.	WEIGHT.	FINENESS.
Five cent piece	77.16 grains	Cu 75%, Ni 25%
Three " "	30.0 "	" " " "
One " "	48. "	Cu 95%, Sn and Zn 5%, (3% Sn, 2% Zn

MEASURES OF WEIGHT AND VOLUME.

AVOIRDUPOIS WEIGHT.

16 Drams (dr.).........make 1 ounce,.........marked oz.

16 Ounces..............make 1 pound,........ " lb.

25 Pounds.............make 1 quarter,....... " qr.

4 Quarters............make 1 hundred-weight " cwt.

20 Hundred-weight.....make 1 ton........... " t.

TROY WEIGHT.

20 Grains (gr)..........make 1 pennyweight... " pwt.

20 Pennyweights.......make 1 ounce......... " oz.

12 Ounces.............make 1 pound......... " lb.

FRENCH OR DECIMAL WEIGHTS.

10 Milligrammes (mg.)	make 1 centigramme	marked cg.
10 Centigrammes	make 1 decigramme	" dcg.
10 Decigrammes	make 1 gramme	" gm.
10 Grammes	make 1 decagramme	" dkg.
10 Decagrammes	make 1 hectogramme	" hg.
10 Hectogrammes	make 1 kilogramme	" kg.
10 Kilogrammes	make 1 myriagramme	" myrg.

The unit of the system is the gramme=15.432349 Troy grains or the weight of 1 c.c. distilled water at 60° F.

ASSAY WEIGHTS.

Multiples	4 Assay Tons=	116.66666 grammes.
	2 Assay Tons=	58.33333 "
Unit...The Assay Ton (marked A. T.)=		29.16666 "
Sub-Divisions	1-3 Assay Ton=	9.7222 "
	1-6 " " =	4.8611 "
	1-10 " " =	2.9166 "
	1-20 " " =	1.4583 "

LIQUID MEASURE.—ENGLISH.

4 Gills (gi.)	make 1 pint	marked pt.
2 Pints	make 1 quart	" qt.
4 Quarts	make 1 gallon	" gal.

LIQUID MEASURE.—FRENCH.

10 Milliliters (ml.)	make 1 centiliter	marked cl.
10 Centiliters	make 1 deciliter	" dcl.
10 Deciliters	make 1 liter	" l.
10 Liters	make 1 decaliter	" dkl.
10 Decaliters	make 1 hectoliter	" hl.
10 Hectoliters	make 1 kiloliter	" kl.

The unit is 1 liter=61.027052 cubic inches, or 1.760773 pints.

CUBIC MEASURE.—ENGLISH.

1728 Cubic inches (c. in.) make 1 cubic foot, marked cu. ft.
27 Cubic feet.......... make 1 cubic yard " c. yd.
16 Cubic feet.......... make 1 cord foot.. " c. ft.
8 Cord ft. or 128 cubic ft. make 1 cord...... " c.

CUBIC MEASURE.—FRENCH.

1000 Cubic centimeters (c. c.) make one cubic decimeter or litré, marked l.

1000 Cubic decimeters make 1 cubic meter or kiloliter, marked kl. or cu. m.

Otherwise the cubic measure is the same as liquid.

COMPARISON OF UNITS.

1 Meter........................ =39.37079 inches
1 Are.......................... =$(39.37079)^2$ square inches
1 Liter........................ =$(3.937079)^3$ cubic inches
1 Pound Avoirdupois........... =7000 grains Troy
1 Pint, English................. =34,65923 cubic inches
1 English ton (2240 lbs.)......... =15,620,000 grains
1 Short ton (2000 lbs.)........... =14,000,000 grains.

SPECIFIC GRAVITY.

The specific gravity of a body is the weight of that body as compared with the weight of an equal volume of another body, assumed as a standard.

The standard for solids and liquids is distilled water; for gases and vapors, dry air and sometimes hydrogen.

All determinations must be made at known temperatures; this for solids and liquids is 60° F.

Gases and vapors may be observed at any known temperature, and the volume reduced by calculation to what it would be at 60° F.

Formulæ for the determination of the specific gravity of solids and liquids:

a. Solids.

1. The substance is heavier than water, and insoluble in it. Weigh it in air and then in water:

Let the weight of the substance in air=W.

Let the weight of the substance in water=W′.

The specific gravity $=\frac{W}{W-W'}$.

2. The substance is heavier than water and insoluble in it:

Fill a flask to any fixed mark on the neck, with water, and weigh; the weight=W′. W=weight of the substance. Place it in the flask and reduce the water to the same level, then weigh the flask, plus substance and water left. Let this weight=W″.

The specific gravity $=\frac{W}{(W+W')-W''}$.

3. The substance is heavier than water, but in fragments; ~~soluble or~~ insoluble. Use the same method as in 2.

4. The substance is heavier than water, but soluble in it: Weigh in some liquid of known specific gravity in which it is insoluble, in place of water. Calculate as follows:

Weight of substance in air=W.

Weight of substance in liquid=W′.

Specific gravity of liquid=S.

Specific gravity of water=1.

The liquid displaced $=W-W'=X$.

Then S is to 1 as X is to $W''=$the water that would have been displaced.

The specific gravity $=\frac{W}{W''}$

5. The substance is insoluble, but lighter than water:

Weight of the substance in air $=W$.

Then weigh in water with a piece of lead attached to sink it. Let this $=W'$.

Weight of the lead alone in water $=W''$

The specific gravity $=\frac{W}{W''-W'+W}$.

6. The substance is soluble, but lighter than water.

Use the process by the flask as in 2, but substitute benzine or turpentine for water.

Weight in air $=W$; in liquid $=W''$. Specific gravity of liquid $=S$. Water $=1$. $W-W'=W''=$ liquid displaced. S is to 1 as W'' is to $X=$ the water that would have been displaced. Specific gravity $=\frac{W}{X}$

b. Liquids.

Three methods may be employed.

1. By the specific gravity bottle. This is a thin glass flask, with a hollow stopper, so as to allow the insertion of a thermometer.

Weight of the flask $=W$.
" " filled with water $=W'$.
" " " " the liquid $=W''$.

Specific gravity $=\frac{W''-W}{W'-W}$.

2. By weighing some body first in water and then in the liquid.

The body weighed in air $=W$.
" " water $=W'$.
" " liquid $=W''$.

Specific gravity $=\frac{W''-W}{W'-W}$.

3. By means of the hydrometer, which is an instrument that placed in a liquid, shows its specific gravity by direct inspection. Its action depends upon the simple principle that a body displaces its own weight of liquid. Hydrometers vary in construction according to the purposes for which they are to be used, but are usually made of light glass tubes with bulbs, blown in a single piece; the weight desired being given by means of small shot or mercury placed in the bulb at the lower end, which is afterwards carefully sealed.

The graduation may be made according to the true scale of specific gravities or arbitrarily; the first is, of course, most desirable and generally employed. For commercial purposes the Baumé scale is often used; it is arbitrary, and is determined by marking the point to which the instrument sinks in pure water "0," and the point to which it sinks in a solution of 15 parts of salt in 85 of water, "15," the interval being divided into 15 equal parts. For specific gravity of gases and vapors, see Watts' Dictionary of Chemistry, Vol. V., page 360.

THERMOMETERS.

Three scales are now in general use. These are:

1. Centigrade—C.	Water freezes at	0°,	boils at	100°.
2. Fahrenheit—F.	" "	32°,	"	212°.
3. Réaumur—R.	" "	0°,	"	80°.

To Convert—F. to C. 5-9 (F.°−32°)=C.°
C. to F. 9-5 C.°+32°=F.°
R. to F. 9-4 R.°+32°=F.°
} Formulæ.

TABLE OF VALUES FOR GRAIN WEIGHTS.

If 240 grains of ore give of fine Metal—Thousandths of 10 grains..................	One Ton of Ore will yield in Troy ounces............	Coin Value per Ton—Gold.	If 240 grains of Ore give of fine Metal—Thousandths of 10 grains..................	One Ton of Ore will yield in Troy ounces............	Coin Value per Ton—Gold.	If 240 grains of Ore gives of fine Metal—Thousandths of 10 grains..................	One Ton of Ore will yield in Troy ounces............	Coin Value per Ton—Gold.
.001	1.21	$ 25.11	7	44.95	$ 929.19	3	88.69	$ 1,883.37
2	2.43	50.23	8	46.17	954.42	4	89.91	1,858.59
3	3.64	75.24	9	47.38	979.43	5	91.12	1,883.60
4	4.86	100.46	.040	48.60	1,004.65	6	92.34	1,908.82
5	6.07	125.48	1	49.81	1,029.66	7	93.55	1,933.83
6	7.29	150.70	2	51.03	1,054.88	8	94.77	1,959.05
7	8.50	175.71	3	52.24	1,079.89	9	95.98	1,984.06
8	9.72	200.93	4	53.46	1.105.11	.080	97.20	2,009.28
9	10.93	325.94	5	54.67	1,130.12	1	98.41	2,034.29
.010	12.15	251.16	6	55.89	1,155.34	2	99.63	2,059.51
1	13.39	276.17	7	57.10	1,180.35	3	100.84	2,084.52
2	14.58	301.39	8	58.32	1.205.57	4	102.06	2,109.74
3	15.79	326.41	9	59.53	1,230.58	5	103.27	2,134.75
4	17.01	351.63	.050	60.75	1,255.80	6	104.49	2,159.97
5	18.22	376.64	1	61.96	1,280.81	7	105.70	2,184.98
6	19.43	401.65	2	63.18	1,306.03	8	106.92	2,210.20
7	20.65	426.87	3	64.39	1,331.04	9	108.13	2,235.21
8	21.86	451.88	4	65.61	1,356.26	.090	109.35	2,260.43
9	43.08	477.10	5	66.82	1,381.27	1	110.56	2,285.44
.020	24.30	502.32	6	68.04	1,406.49	2	111.78	2,310.66
1	35.51	527.34	7	69.25	1,431.50	3	112.99	2,335.67
2	26.73	552.56	8	70.47	1,456.72	4	114.21	2,360.89
3	27.94	577.57	9	71.68	1,481.73	5	115.42	2,385.90
4	29.16	602.79	.060	72.90	1,506.95	6	116.64	2,411.12
5	30.37	627.80	1	74.11	1,531.96	7	117.85	2,436.13
6	31.59	653.02	2	75.33	1,557.18	8	119.07	2,461.35
7	32.80	678.03	3	76.54	1,582.19	9	120.28	2,486.36
8	34.02	703.25	4	77.76	1,607.41	.100	121.50	2,511.62
9	35.23	728.26	5	78.97	1,632.42	.200	243.00	5,023.25
.030	36.45	753.48	6	80.19	1,657.64	.300	364.50	7,131.77
1	37.66	778.50	7	81.40	1,682.65	.400	486.00	10,046.50
2	38.88	803.72	8	82.62	1,707.87	.500	607.50	15,558.12
3	40.09	828.73	9	83.83	1,732.88	.600	729.00	14,263.55
4	41.31	853.95	.070	85.05	1,758.13	.700	850.50	17,581.37
5	42.52	978.96	1	86.26	1,783.14	.800	972.00	20,093.00
6	43.74	904.18	2	87.48	1,808.36	.900	1,093.50	22,604.61
						1000	1,215.00	25,116.25

MULTIPLICATION TABLE FOR GOLD.

20.67×1=20.67	20.67×4= 82.68	20.67×7=144.69
20.67×2=41.34	20.67×5=103.35	20.67×8=165.36
20.60×3=62.01	20.67×6=124.02	20.67×9=186.03

EXAMPLE.—Suppose an ore gave an assay 218.6 oz., then ....

4134
2067
6536
12402, added, will give

$13080.404 per ton of 2,000 lbs.

See Errata

GENERAL STYLE OF REPORT.

(Certificate.)

New York, ... 187

DEAR SIR:

The sample of ....

From ....

Marked ....

submitted to me for examination, contains ....

Very respectfully,

To

QUANTITATIVE REPORT.

(For Reference.)

New York, ... 187

Report of

Analysis of

Determination of

Grammes taken:

Method of Analysis.

Precipitates.	Actual Weights.	Constituents.	Calculated Weights.	Percentages.	Theoretical Percentages.

Special Remarks

TIN—CRUCIBLE ASSAY.

Ore Assayed.	Charge.	No. of Assay.	TIME.			SLAG.		BUTTON.				True Per Cent.	Remarks.
			To Fusion.	After Fusion.	Total.	Color.	Character.	Character.	Weight.	Per Cent.	Average Per Cent.		

Dated, Signed,

For lead, antimony, etc., simply change the name of the metal.

IRON—CRUCIBLE ASSAY.

Ore—Marked
Min. Character
Composition
Alumina per cent.
Silica "
Lime "

	No. 1.	No. 2.
Charge—Ore	Gms.	Gms.
Silica	"	"
Lime	"	"
Glass	"	"
Kaolin	"	"
Fluorspar	"	"
In fire—	Hours.	Hours.
Slag, Color / Appearance		
Button, Wt. / Character	Gms.	Gms.

Remarks

REPORT.

Assay
No. 1 per cent Iron.
No. 2 " " "
Average " " "

Sample Averaged on Ore
Dated
No. Signed

SILVER AND GOLD—CRUCIBLE ASSAY.

Ore—Marked

Min. Character

Reducing Power Gms.= Gms. Lead.

	No. 1.	No. 2.
Charge—Ore	A. T.	A. T.
Litharge	"	"
Carb. Potash or Soda	"	"
Borax, Anhydrous	"	"
Silica	"	"
Charcoal or Argol	Gms.	Gms.
Nitre	"	"
Salt	"	"
In fire—to fusion	Mts.	Mts.
after fusion	"	"
Slag, Color		
Appearance		
Lead Button, Wt.	Gms.	Gms.
Character	"	"
Scorification—Fluxes		
Wt. after 1st	Gms.	Gms.
" " 2d	"	"
Cupellation—Silver and Gold	Mgs.	Mgs.
Gold in Ore	"	"
Silver	"	"
Silver in Litharge	"	"
Silver in Ore	"	"

Remarks

REPORT.

Contained in 2,000 lbs. Ore

Assay	Gold	Silver	Total	Gold	Silver	Total
No. 1.	oz.	oz.	oz.	$	$	$
No. 2.	oz.	oz.	oz.	$	$	$
Average	oz.	oz.	oz.	$	$	$

Sample Averaged on Ore

Dated

No. Signed

SILVER AND GOLD—SCORIFICATION ASSAY.

Ore—Marked

Min. Character

	No. 1.	No. 2.
Charge—Ore	A. T.	A. T.
Test Lead	Gms.	Gms.
Borax (Anhydrous)	"	"
Silica or Glass	"	"
No. of Scorifiers	'	
Scorification		
Slag—Color		
Appearance		
Button—Character		
Weight		
" after 2d Scor.	Gms.	Gms.
" " 3d "	"	"
" " 4th "	"	"
" " 5th "	"	"
Cupellation	Mgs.	Mgs.
Gold in Ore	"	"
Silver	"	"
Silver in Test Lead	"	"
Silver in Ore	"	"

Remarks

REPORT.

Contained in 2,000 lbs. Ore.

Assay	Gold	Silver	Total	Gold	Silver	Total
No. 1.	oz.	oz.	oz.	$	$	$
Fo. 2.	oz.	oz.	oz.	$	$	$
Average	oz.	oz.	oz.	$	$	$

Sample Averaged on Ore

Dated

No. Signed

GOLD BULLION ASSAY.

Alloy—Marked

	No. 1.	No. 2.
Copper Assay		
Bullion	Thds.	Thds.
Lead	Gms.	Gms.
Gold and Silver	Thds.	Thds.
Base metal	"	"
Assay proper		
Cupellation		
Bullion	Mgs.	Mgs.
Silver	"	"
Lead	Gms.	Gms.
Copper	"	"
Parting		
Cornet	Mgs.	Mgs.
Silver retained	"	"
Gold	"	"

Remarks

REPORT.

Assay	Gold.	Silver.	Base Metal.
No. 1.	Fine	Thds.	Thds.
No. 2.	"	"	"
Average	"	"	"

Dated

No. Signed

SILVER BULLION ASSAY.

Alloy—Marked

	No. 1.	No. 2.
Cupellation		
Bullion	Mgs.	Mgs.
Lead	Gms.	Gms.
Silver	Mgs.	Mgs.
Correction for Loss	"	"
Fineness		
Volumetric Assay		
Bullion	Gms.	Gms.
Normal Salt solution	1000. Dgs.	1000. Dgs.
Decimal " "	"	"
Total	"	"
Decimal Silver solution	"	"
Total Salt	"	"
Equiv in Silver	Gms.	Gms.
Fineness	Thds.	Thds.

Re

REPORT.

Assay	Silver.	Copper, &c.
No. 1	Fine.	Thds.
No. 2	"	"
Average	"	"

Dated

No. Signed

PROBLEMS AND QUESTIONS.

1. What would be the best method of assaying a poor argentiferous sulphide of antimony for the silver ?

2. Explain the derivation of the assay ton, and calculate its weight for England and the United States.

3. An iron ore contains by analysis—

Silica........25.96 per cent.		Calculate the charge for Percy's slag.
Alumina..... 6.92	"	
Lime........ 2.72	"	
Magnesia.... 4.87	"	

4. What is the theory of the lead assay ?

5. Describe the operations and the theory of the scorification assay for silver ores.

6. What would be the best method of treating a pure iron pyrites containing gold ?

7. Mention the reagents employed in the silver crucible assay and the action of each.

8. Given an ore containing, gold .002 per cent.; silver, .005 per cent.; which has a reducing power of 2=3.6 of lead. Calculate the best charge for assay and give the value in ounces and dollars per ton.

9. 50 gms. of an ore, sifted, gave 2.59 scales and 47.40 gms. siftings. The scales, melted down with lead, gave a button of 35 gms. 10 gms. of this button yielded, silver 4.5 mgs.; gold 1.3 mgs. $\frac{1}{8}$ A. T. of the siftings yielded silver 6.95 mgs.; gold 1.85 mgs. Required the ounces and dollars per A. T. of the original ore.

10. An alloy cupelled gave .985 gms. of silver in one gramme. Added in the volumetric test. Normal salt, 100 c.c. Decimal silver, 5 c.c. 99.5 c.c. normal salt=1 gm. of pure silver. Calculate the weight of the alloy taken for volumetric assay and the fineness.

11. Calculate the charges for the following reducing powers, the charge of ore being one assay ton: (2 gms.=16.5), (2 gms.=.42), (2 gms.=5.2), (2 gms.=1.2).

12. An ore contains:

Silver	2.5 oz.	per ton.
Gold	5.8 "	
Lead	15 per cent.	

Also sulphur, antimony and iron in quantity. How should it be assayed ?

13. One gramme of an alloy, cupelled and parted, gave silver, 984.2 mgs.; gold, 8.4 mgs. Wet assay.

Added normal salt	100 c.c.
Decime salt	13 "
" silver	3 "

Strength of normal, 101.2 c.c.=1 gramme pure silver. Calculate the fineness of the bullion.

14. Describe the reactions that take place in the nickel and cobalt assay.

15. Name eighteen principal reagents for the various assays, giving formulæ.

16. Describe the advantages and disadvantages of the tin assay, lead assay, iron assay, etc.

17. Mention the ores of lead, tin, iron, silver and gold.

REFERENCES ON ASSAYING.

Barstow Wm.: Sulphurets; treatment, etc.; San Francisco, 1867.

Bodemann Th. u. Bruno Kerl. Anleitung zur Berg. und Hütten-Männischen Probirkunst; Clausthal, 1857; 2d edition.

Bodemann Th. and Bruno Kerl: Treatise on the Assaying of Lead, Copper, Silver, Gold and Mercury; translated by W. A. Goodyear; New York, 1865.

Blossom T. M.: On Gold, Silver and Iron; see American Chemist for 1870.

Budge J.: Practical Miners' Guide; London, 1866.

Byland A.: Assay of Gold and Silver Wares.

Kerl Wm.: A Practical Treatise on Metallurgy; edited by Wm. Crooks and Ernst Rohrig.

Lieber O. M.: The Assayers' Guide.

Mitchell John: Manual of Practical Assaying; edited by William Crooks; New York, 1872.

Mitchell John: Manual of Practical Assaying; London, 1868.

Overman Frederick: Practical Mineralogy, Assaying and Mining; Philadelphia, 1863.

Silversmith Julius: Handbook for Miners, Metallurgists and Assayers.

Knapp F.: Chemical Technology.

Watt Henry: Dictionary of Chemistry; London, 1866–72. See under the heads of the different metals.

Besides the above, almost all works on the chemistry of the metals treat more or less of the assay of the same.

The books mentioned have been given independent of any merit; there are doubtless many others equally good, which the author has not met with.

APPENDIX.

MANIPULATION, FORMULÆ AND CALCULATION.

The various operations of weighing, mixing, charging, etc., have already been described under their appropriate heads; and it only remains to give a few hints on operations peculiar or necessary in the performance of assays in the wet way, or analyses.

PRECIPITATION.—This operation is the sudden conversion of a dissolved body into the solid state; either by a modification of the solvent, or decomposition with the formation of a new compound.

The separation of a precipitate is generally aided by the action of heat and agitation.

Porcelain and glass vessels will be found the best.

In adding the necessary reagent pour in carefully until the precipitate ceases to form, unless otherwise directed.

FILTRATION.—This operation has for its object the separation of the solid particles suspended in a fluid, from the same. Various substances might be used as a filter; but the best is unsized paper, which is prepared for the purpose by cutting a circular form and then folding it into halves and quarters, so that it will just fit into a funnel, and not project above the rim of the same. For quantitative work, the prepared Swedish filter paper will be found the best; it should be cut into circular pieces as described; which should be of a constant size to suit the funnels; and the ash left by burning one of the same carefully determined. As a rule, it will be found best to moisten the paper before filtering with water, and to pour the fluid portion through first.

DECANTATION.—This is simply a substitute for filtration; the clear liquor being poured off from the precipitate. To effect this the vessel should be inclined gently, and the liquid permitted to run down a glass rod, held against the spout of the same.

Washing.—This is best effected by using a glass flask, fitted with a cork, in which is inserted two glass tubes, one reaching to the bottom of the flask, and bent to any desired angle on the outside, the end being drawn to a point. The second tube reaches to just below the cork, and is also bent on the outside, but not drawn to a point; by blowing on this tube the water is expelled through the first. Warm water will be found the most effective. The completeness of the washing may be tested by evaporating a small portion of the filtrate on platinum foil, and noting the residue.

Evaporation.—Porcelain dishes are the best for this operation; but if the solution is to be evaporated to dryness it should be conducted over a water bath. A sand bath may be used, but care should be taken to prevent loss by spattering.

Ignition.—The washed precipitate, after being dried, is ignited to completely expel all moisture, or convert it into a constant or weighable substance. This is best conducted by transferring to a weighed porcelain crucible, and burning the filter paper over it, either on the inverted cover, or by wrapping it in a coil of platinum wire and holding it over the crucible. The ash should be heated until white, or nearly so. The whole operation must be conducted over a piece of glazed paper until the filter paper is burnt, after which the crucible and contents should be heated over a burner or lamp; gently at first. After ignition the crucible and contents should be cooled in a desiccator, to avoid absorption of moisture from the air.

Formulæ and Calculation.—The general methods of calculation have been given under the various assays, but it will be well to bear in mind the following:

1st. The equivalent of the compound found is to the equivalent of its constituent which is sought; as the weight of the compound is to the weight of the constituent.

2d. The weight of the substance taken for assay is to the weight of the constituent sought as one hundred is to the per cent. of the same.

The equivalents will be found in the table on page 14. The equivalent of a compound being equal to the sum of the equivalents of the constituents of the same. Thus, H_2SO_4 (sulphuric acid) is equal to 2+32+64=98. The equivalent of hydrogen (H), being 1. Sulphur (S)=32. Oxygen (O)=16. Two parts of hydrogen being 2; four parts of oxygen=64.

BLOWPIPE ANALYSIS, APPARATUS AND REAGENTS.

The assayer will find that a knowledge of the proper use of the blowpipe will prove a great saving of time and labor, by enabling him to more fully understand the character of many substances presented for assay, which he could not otherwise determine save by qualitative analysis.

The first and most important thing in blowpipe analysis is to learn to blow and breathe at the same time, without removing the mouth from the instrument or interrupting the blast; this can be done by filling the mouth with air and breathing through the nose, expelling some of the air into the mouth at each breath.

The blowpipe flame consists of two distinct portions. 1st. The outside or oxydizing flame; 2d. The inner blue cone, the point of which is the hottest part of the flame. Its action is reducing. This flame is obtained by putting the point of the blowpipe about one-quarter of the way into the lamp flame. The true reducing flame is entirely yellow, the blowpipe point being held just outside of the lamp flame.

The substance to be tested should be finely powdered and treated:

1st. On charcoal.

This is best done by making a small hole in the right hand corner of the coal, nearest the lamp, placing a little of the substance in the same and testing first with the oxydizing and then with the reducing flame, noting the action of each and the color of the coating formed, etc.

The holes in the charcoal should be bored on the edge of the grain to avoid splintering. Blow across the coal.

2d. If the substance treated gives off volatile fumes on charcoal, test a little of it in a closed and open tube successively, first alone, and then in the closed tube with a little carbonate of soda. Note the coating formed and the color and order of the fumes.

3d. Test the substance with the borax, salt of phosphorus, and soda beads successively; this may be done on platinum wire or, if the substance be metallic, on charcoal. To make the proper sized bead, bend the end of the wire into a loop on the point of a sharp pencil, dip it into the reagent and melt before the blowpipe until a clear, good bead is formed, then add the substance and heat, first in the oxydizing and then in the reducing flame.

4th. Apply special tests, as the color of the flame, the action of nitrate of cobalt on the coat formed on charcoal; adding the cobalt solution and then heating. If the substance is not metallic the color of the flame can best be noted by testing in the platinum pointed forceps; moistening the material with hydrochloric acid, and bringing it into the tip of the blue cone of the blowpipe flame.

To get the methods of performing the above operations the following substances will serve as type examples:

To test blowing and flames, oxide of manganese and molybdic acid.

To test on charcoal, lead and antimony.

To test in the matrass or closed tube, cinnabar and arsenic.

To test in the open tube, stibnite and sulphur.

To test with the beads.

Borax bead, oxide of copper.

Salt of phosphorus, the same and sesquioxide of iron.

Soda bead, manganese and chromium.

CHARACTERISTIC TESTS.

Potassa, colors the flame violet; best seen through a blue glass.

Soda, reddish-yellow flame.

Lithia, carmine-red flame.

Ammonia, colors red litmus-paper blue, pungent odor.

Baryta, burnt with alcohol gives a yellowish-green flame.

Strontia, crimson flame.

Lime, colors the flame feebly red, becomes caustic and glows when heated.

Magnesia, gives with nitrate of cobalt a pale flesh-color, after long blowing.

Alumina, gives a fine blue color with nitrate of cobalt.

Silica, in Sp. Ph. bead gives a semi-transparent skeleton floating in the bead.

Oxide of antimony, on charcoal, is reduced, and gives white fumes and coat and greenish-blue flame.

Arsenious acid, with soda on charcoal, gives white fumes and garlic odor.

Oxide of bismuth, on charcoal, is reduced to metal, and gives an orange-yellow color.

Oxide of cadmium, coats the coal with a reddish-brown powder and variegated tarnish.

Oxide of chromium, with soda in the O. F. gives a yellow glass; in R. F., green on cooling.

Oxide of cobalt, on charcoal becomes magnetic. With borax and S. Ph. beads, smalt-blue glass.

Oxide of copper, metallic button on charcoal. With borax bead, green glass, blue when cold; red in R. F.

Oxide of gold, with borax on coal easily reducible to metal.

Oxide of iron, on coal becomes magnetic. Borax bead, red to yellow on cooling; in R. F., bottle-green.

Oxide of lead, reducible to metal on charcoal with sulphur-yellow coat and blue flame.

Oxide of manganese, with soda, on cooling bluish-green. With borax, amethyst bead, colorless in reducing flame.

Oxide of mercury, volatile on charcoal, metallic mirror with soda in closed tube.

Molybdic acid, with S. Ph., yellowish-green, and colorless when cold. The bead on coal becomes green on cooling.

Oxide of nickel, on charcoal, yields a magnetic powder. Borax bead, reddish-brown.

Oxide of silver, on charcoal, reducible to metal. With borax, opalescent or milk-white glass.

Oxide of tin, reducible on charcoal to metal with yellow coat, white when cold. With cobalt solution in O. F., gives a bluish-green color.

Titanic acid, with salt of phosphorus bead in R. F., a fine violet color.

Oxide of zinc, yellow coat on coal, white when cold. With cobalt solution, green in O. F.

Chlorine, with oxide of copper in borax bead a fine azure blue flame.

Iodine, with soda, or better, bi-sulphate of potash; in matrass, violet fumes.

Bromine, with bi-sulphate of potash in matrass, reddish-yellow vapors.

Fluorine, etches glass when mixed with a little sulphuric acid.

Carbonic acid, acid reaction, turns lime-water white.

Sulphur, burns on charcoal with a blue flame with odor of sulphurous acid; better in open tube.

SCHEME FOR BLOWPIPE ANALYSIS.

The substance may contain As, Sb, S, Se, Fe, Mn, Cu, Co, Ni, Pb, Bi, Ag, Au, Hg, Zn, Cd, Sn, Cl, Br, I, CO_2, SiO_2, HNO_3, H_2O, &c.

---

1. Treat on Ch. in the O. F, to find volatile substances, such as As, Sb, S, Se, Pb, Bi, Ag, Zn, Cd., &c.

---

a. If there are volatile substances present, form a coating and test it with S.Ph. and tin on Ch. for Sb; or to distinguish between Pb and Bi.

b. If there are no volatile substances present, divide a part of the substance into three portions and proceed as in A.

Sb. gives gray bead, clear on long blowing; Bi. clear and colorless when hot, blackish-gray and opaque on cooling; Pb. cloudy and dark, but never quite opaque. In testing for Bi. the antimony must be driven off first.

If Sb. is present it is not necessary to look for Bi and *vice versa.* These two substances are very rarely found together. The same is true of Pb and Bi.

2. If As, Sb, S, Se are present, roast a large quantity thoroughly on Ch. in the O. F. Divide the substance into three portions, and proceed as in A.

A. Treatment of the First Portion. —Dissolve a very small quantity in borax on platinum wire in the O. F. and observe the color produced. Various colors will be formed by the combination of the oxides. Saturate the bead and shake it off into a porcelain dish.

a. Treat the bead on Ch. with a small piece of lead, silver or gold, in a strong R. F.

b. Fe, Mn, Co, &c., remain in the bead.

If the bead spreads out on the Ch., it must be collected to a globule by continued blowing.

Make a borax bead on platinum wire and dissolve it in *some* of the fragments of the bead, reserving the rest for accidents.

c. Ni, Cu, Ag, Au, Sn, Pb, Bi, are reduced and collected by the lead button.

Remove the button from the bead while hot, or by breaking the latter when cold, on the anvil between paper; carefully preserving all the fragments.

d. If Co is present, the bead will be blue. If a large amount of Fe is present, add a little borax to prove the presence or absence of Co, by diluting the bead, the cobalt color being more intense. If Mn is present, the bead when treated on platinum wire in the O. F. will become dark violet or black.	*e.* If only Fe and Mn and no Co be present, the bead will be almost colorless. Look here for Cr, Ti, Mo. and W. Mo will give a cloudy-brown or black with the borax bead in the R. F.; owing to the molybdic acid being reduced.

f. Treat the button *c* on Ch. in the O. F. until all the lead, &c., is driven off, Ni, Cu, Ag, and Au remaining behind.

g. Treat the residue on Ch. in O. F. with S.Ph. bead, removing the button while the bead is hot.

h. If Ni and Cu are present, the bead will be green when cold. If Ni only—yellow. If Cu only—blue.

Prove Cu by treating the S.Ph. bead with tin on Ch. in the R. F., the bead becomes red on cooling.

Ni and Cu may be separated by fusing them with a gold button of equal weight and oxidizing with borax or S.Ph. The Ni is dissolved first in the borax glass.

i. For Ag and Au make the special test No. 8.

B. TREATMENT OF THE SECOND PORTION.—Drive off the volatile substances in the O. F. on Ch. Treat with the R. F., or mix with soda, and then treat with the R. F., for Zn, Cd, Sn. If a white coating is formed, test with cobalt solution and observe the color. Tin gives greenish-blue, zinc, green. If Zn is found, it is not necessary to look for Sn, and *vice versa*, as they very rarely occur together. Cd. gives a brown coat and variegated tarnish.

C. TREATMENT OF THE THIRD PORTION.—Dissolve some the substance in S.Ph. on platinum wire in O. F., observing whether SiO_2 is present or not, and test for Mn with nitrate of potassa, and soda.

3. Test for As with soda on Ch. in the R. F., or with *dry* soda in a closed tube. On charcoal it gives garlic odor; in the tube, a metallic mirror.

4. Dissolve in S.Ph. on platinum wire in the O. F. (if the substance is not metallic and does not contain any S.) and test for Sb on Ch. with tin in the R. F. See 1, *a*.

5. Test for Se on charcoal; it gives a horse-radish odor.

6. In the absence of Se, fuse with soda in the R. F. and and test for S on silver foil. By moistening the fused mass and letting it stand on the foil the latter turns black if S be present. In the presence of Se test in open tube.

7. Test for Hg with *dry* soda in a closed tube; a metallic mirror is formed.

8. Mix some of the substance with assay lead and borax glass and fuse on Ch. in the R. F. Cupel the lead button for Ag. Test with nitric acid for Au, dissolving the silver.

9. Test for Cl and I with a bead of S.Ph. saturated with oxide of copper. Cl gives blue flame; I, intense green.

10. Test for Br with bi-sulphate of potassa in a matrass, gives brownish-yellow fumes.

11. Test for H_2O in a closed tube; drops collect on the interior.

12. Test on platinum wire, or in platinum pointed forceps, for coloration of the flame.

13. Test for CO_2 with hydrochloric acid, letting the gas pass over lime water.

14. Test for HNO_3 with bi-sulphate of potassa in a matrass; yellow colored fumes, and acid reaction.

15. Test for Te in an open tube; forms a grayish-white sublimate which fuses to clear, transparent drops when strongly heated. Te burns with a bluish-green flame.

The above scheme is essentially the same as the one used by the students of the School of Mines, New York, prepared by Prof. Thos. Egleston. A few changes have been made so as to render reference to works on blowpipe analyses unnecessary.

The abbreviations O. F., R. F., Ch., and S. Ph., stand respectively for oxidizing flame, reducing flame, charcoal, and salt of phosphorus,

BLOWPIPE APPARATUS.

Blowpipe, with platinum jet, in three pieces, with cylinder to catch the moisture.

Lamp, for blowpipe, with swivel and stand, four pieces.

Lamp, alcohol, with brass cover ground to fit, for lighting large lamp.

Forceps, steel, nickel plated (Raynor's), for testing color of flames.

Forceps, brass, to handle small buttons, beads, etc.

Forceps, steel, for lamp, to raise wick with.

Plyers, cutting, for clipping minerals, sampling, etc.

Plyers, flat nose (nippers) for quantitative work, handling lead buttons.

Holder, cupel with two cups and one mould, for cupelling lead buttons.

Holder, charcoal, with platinum ring and shield, for quantitative work.

Holder for evaporating dish, with triangle, for parting, making solutions, etc.

Holder for chimney, to concentrate the flame of alcohol lamp.

Holder for platinum wire, with six wires, for making bead tests.

Holder for matrass, to hold tubes, etc.

Hammer, for breaking slag, pounding buttons, etc.

Anvil, " " " "

Borer, charcoal, club shape, to make holes in charcoal and coals.

Borer, charcoal, four-cornered, to enlarge coal crucibles for quantitative work.

Borer, charcoal, with spatula, for quantitative work, useful in boring out coals.

Capsule, mixing, brass, gilded, to mix charges for quantitative work in.

Spatula, mixing, steel, for mixing charges.

Spoons, ivory, two, for measuring out reagents, etc.

Brush, assay button, for cleaning buttons before weighing.

Charcoal saw, to shape charcoal.

Tray, for coal, for quantitative work, mostly.

Tray, for dirt.

Scissors, for lamp, to trim, etc.

Knife, small, with long thin blade.

Magnifier, with two lenses, to examine minerals.

Magnet, bar with chisel edge, to test for iron, nickel and cobalt.

Form for paper cylinders, for quantitative work.

Test lead measure, " "

Small camel's hair brushes, to clean up with..

Moulds for making crucibles, coals, and capsules.

Steel mortar for crushing minerals.

Agate mortar for pulverizing.

A small glass wash bottle.

Small platinum spoon for fusions.

Scales for quantitative work; a bullion balance will do as well; also a measuring scale for buttons. Glass matrasses, closed and open tubes, porcelain dishes and capsules, and clay cylinders for coal crucibles.

For quantitative work the assayer will also require:

Coal crucibles and capsules.

Clay " "

Square coals and covers.

BLOWPIPE REAGENTS.

Carbonate of soda, pure and dry.

Neutral oxalate of potassa, pulverized.

Cyanide of potassium, pulverized.
Iodide of potassium, "
Borax and borax glass, "
Salt of phosphorus (phosphate of soda and ammonia).
Nitre (crystals).
Bi-sulphate of potassa, pulverized.
Vitrified boracic acid, in small fragments.
Nitrate of cobalt in solution.
Test lead, finely granulated.
Tin, in foil best.
Iron. Wire or pieces of ½″ to 1″ long,
Gold, in foil.
Arsenic, metallic,
Test papers, blue and red litmus.
Salt, pulverized and dry.
Fluorspar, fine and dry.
Silica, ignited and white.
Oxide of copper.
Chloride of silver, in paste.
Starch meal.
Graphite, fine and pure.
Concentrated sulphuric, nitric, and muriatic acids.
Acetic acid.
Carbonate of ammonia in powder.
Charcoal cut in blocks $3'' \times \frac{3}{4}'' \times \frac{1}{2}''$.
Sifted and washed bone-ash.

GENERAL REMARKS.

To clean a dirty platinum point hold it in the flame of the alcohol lamp with the platinum pointed forceps.

To clean platinum wires, heat and plunge into muriatic acid.

To break small pieces of mineral, wrap in paper or cloth before hammering.

To trim the wick of blowpipe lamp, cut even with the lamp and raise with one point of the steel forceps.

CHEMICAL APPARATUS AND REAGENTS.

(Qualitative and Quantitative.)

APPARATUS.

GLASSWARE.

Lipped Beakers, nests of six.
Plain " " "
Flasks, 1 oz.
" 2 "
" 4 "
" 6 "
" 8 "
" 16 " (pint)
" 24 "
" 3 Litres.
" 50 c.c. (measured).
" 100 " "
" 200 " "
" ½ Litre, "
" 1 " "
" Specific gravity.
Pipettes, 10 c.c.
" 100 "
Gay Lussac Burettes.
Carb. Acid Apparatus (Wetherell's).
Carb. Acid Apparatus (Geissler's).
Wash Bottles, 4 oz.
" " 8 "
" " 16 " (pint).
" " 24 "
Wash Bottle Tubes.
Funnels, No. 1 (1½ inch).
" No. 2 (2¾ ")
" No. 3 (3¼ ")
" No. 4 (4 ")
" No. 5 (5 ")
" No. 6 (6 ")
Watch Glasses.
Convex Covers, 3 inch.
" " 3¼ "
Convex Covers, 4 inch.
" " 4½ "
" " 5 "
" " 5½ "
" " 6 "
Flat Covers, 3 "
" " 4 "
" " 5 "
" " (thick) 5 "
Pieces Blue Glass.
Desiccators (covered).
Bottles, corked, 1 oz.
" " 2 "
" " 3 "
" " 4 "
" " 6 "
" " 8 "
" Glass stoppered, ½ oz.
" " " 1 to 6 "
Glass tubes
Glass Rods.
Calcic Chloride Tubes.
Funnel Tubes.
" " (stop cocks).
Ignition Bulb Tubes.
U Tubes, set of four.
" " No. 1 (5½ inch).
" " No. 2 (6 ")
" " No. 3 (12 ")
Test Tubes, 4 inch.
" " 6 "
" " 7 "
" " 8 "
Specimen Tubes.
Retorts, ¼ Litre.
" ½ "
" 1 "
" 2 "

Porcelain.

Porcelain Mortars, 4½ inch.
" " 5 "
" " Ex. Pestle for.
" Evap. Dishes, nests of 6.
" " " 12 inch.
" Casseroles, 3½ "
" " 4 "
" " 4½ "
" " 5 "
" " 5½ "
" Crucibles, 1½ "
" " 1¾ "
" " 2 "

Paper.

Packages Cut Filters, 3 inch.
" " 3½ "
" " 4 "
" " 4½ "
" " 5 "
" " 5½ "
" " 6 "
" " 7 "
" " 8 "
" " 9 "
Sheets Swedish Paper.
" Glazed Paper.
Note Books.

Metal.

Ring Stands.
Files, Triangular.
Steel Forceps.
" " (bent).
Wire Triangles.
" " (covered) 2 inch.
" " " 3 "
Scissors.
Pieces Wire Gauze.
Bunsen Burners.
Water Baths.
Watch Glass Clips.
Sand Baths.
Set Filter Patterns.
Platinum Foils, 1½ inch.
" " 3 "
" Wire, 10 feet.
" Crucible, ¾ oz.
Gas Stoves.
Blowpipes.
Clamps.

Sundries.

Filter Stands.
Test Tube Racks.
Rubber Tubing, black, ⅛ inch.
" " white, ⅛ "
" " " ¼ "
" Corks.
Sponge Probangs.
Horn Spatulas, 4 inch.
" " 5 "
" " 6 "
Towels.
Test Tube Brushes.
Clay Chimneys.

REAGENTS.

Hydrochloric Acid (concent.), HCl. Hydrochloric Acid (dilute), HCl. Nitric Acid (concent.), HNO_3. Nitric Acid (dilute), HNO_3. Sulphuric Acid (concent.), H_2SO_4. Sulphuric Acid (dilute), H_2SO_4. Hydrosulphuric Acid, H_2S. Potassic Hydrate, KHO. Sodic Carbonate, Na_2CO_3. Ammonic Hydrate, $(NH_4)HO$. Ammonic Carbonate, $(NH_4)_2CO_3$. Ammonic Chloride, $(NH_4)Cl$. Ammonic Sulphide, $(NH_4)_2S$.

Ammonic Oxalate, $(NH_4)_2C_2O_4$. Baric Chloride, $BaCl_2$. Hydro-Di-Sodic Phosphate, Na_2HPO_4. Potassic Ferrocyanide, $K_4Cfy=4KCy,FeCy_2$. Potassic Ferricyanide, $K_6Cfdy=6KCy,Fe_2Cy_6$. Ferric Chloride, Fe_2Cl_6. Acetic Acid, $HC_2H_3O_2$. Calcic Sulphate, $CaSo_4$. Mercuric Chloride, $HgCl_2$. Stannous Chloride, $SnCl_2$. Sodic Acetate, $NaC_2H_3O_2$. Ammonic Sulphate, $(NH_4)_2SO_4$. Potassic Dichromate, K_2CrO_4. CrO_3. Magnesic Sulphate, $MgSO_4$. Lime Water, CaH_2O_2. Calcic Chloride, $CaCl_2$. Plumbic Acetate, $Pb(C_2H_3O_2)_2$. Indigo Solution, $C_8H_5NO.SO_3$. Argentic Nitrate, $AgNO_3$. Platinic Chloride, $PtCl_4$. Ammonic Molybdate, $(NH_4)_2MoO_4$ (+nitric Acid). Ammonic Sulphocyanide, $(NH_4)CNS$. Baric Carbonate, $BaCO_3$. Sodic Carbonate (dry), Na_2CO_3. Borax (crystallized), $2NaBO_2.B_2O_3+10H_2O$. Phosphorus Salt (crystallized), $Na(NH_4)HPO_4+4H_2O$. Sodic Nitrate (crystals), $NaNO_3$. Potassic Cyanide (powder), $KCy=KCN$. Cobaltic Nitrate, $Co(NO_3)_2$. Ferrous Sulphate (crystals), $FeSO_4$. Test Papers (blue, red and yellow). Common Sulphuric Acid, H_2SO_4. Common Hydrochloric Acid, HCl.

EXTRA REAGENTS.—Alphabetical order:

Alcohol (absolute), $C_2H_5.OH$. Alcohol (common), $C_2H_5.OH$. Ammonic Fluoride, $(NH_4)F$. Arsenic (metallic), As. Battery Acid (dilute), H_2SO_4.1-10. Battery Fluid, 10 parts H_2O; 3 parts H_2SO_4; 1 part $K_2Cr_2O_7$. Benzol (pure), C_6H_6. Benzol (common), C_6H_6. Bromine Water, Br. Chlorine Water, Cl. Chloroform, $CHCl_3$. Distilled Water, H_2O. Iron (wire and plate), Fe. Lead (bar and foil), Pb. Mercury, Hg. Nitro-Hydrochloric Acid (aqua regia), HNO_3+3HCl. Oxalic Acid (crystals), $H_2C_2O_4$. Potassic Iodide (crystals), KI. Potassic Carbonate (dry), K_2CO_3. Potassic Nitrate, KNO_3. Potassic Nitrite, KNO_2. Potassic Chlorate, $KClO_3$. Potassic Permanganate (crystals), $K_2Mn_2O_8$, Silver (foil), Ag. Sodic Acetate (crystals), $NaC_2H_3O_2$. Sulphur (roll), S. Sulphur (flowers), S. Zinc (bar and sheet), Zn.

ZETTNOW'S SCHEME FOR QUALITATIVE ANALYSIS WITHOUT THE USE OF H_2S OR $(NH_4)HS$.

ARRANGED BY H. CARRINGTON BOLTON, PH. D.

For the Students of the School of Mines, Columbia College.

Add hydrochloric acid to the solution, wash, and filter.

- *Precipitate.* Boil with water and filter.
  - *Solution.* Add H_2SO_4.
    - *Precipitate* **Pb**
  - *Residue.* Treat with $(NH_4)HO$.
    - *Solution.* Add HNO_3.
      - *Precipitate* **Ag**
    - *Residue* turns gray or black **Hg**
- *Filtrate.* Add excess of dilute H_2SO_4 and wash on filter.
  - *Precipitate.* Agitate with considerable cold water and filter.
    - *Filtrate.* Add excess of $(NH_4)_2C_2O_4$.
      - *Precipitate* **Ca**
    - *Residue.* Add $(NH_4)HO$ and $(NH_4)_2C_4H_4O_6$ digest and filter.
      - *Residue.* Boil with Na_2CO_3, filter, wash, dissolve on filter with HCl, neutralize filtrate with $(NH_4)HO$, and divide into two parts.
        - *1st Half.* Add excess of solution of $SrSO_4$.
          - *Precipitate* **Ba**
        - *Second Half.* Add excess of $H_2Si_3Fl_6$ and alcohol. Shake, filter, dilute with water, expel alcohol by evaporation, add solution of $CaSO_4$, and after one or two minutes a precipitate **Sr**
      - *Filtrate.* Add $H(C_2H_3O_2)$ and K_2CrO_4.
        - *Precipitate* **Pb**
  - *Filtrate.* Divide the solution into two unequal parts, ¼ and ¾.
    - To ¼ add BaH_2O_2 and boil.
      - *Volatilized* $(NH_4)_2O$. Test gas with HCl and litmus.
      - *Solution.* Add excess of $(NH_4)_2CO_3$ and $(NH_4)_2C_2O_4$ warm, filter, evaporate to dryness, and ignite residue. Test on platinum wire in colorless flame; intense yellow color indicates **Na.** Violet color seen through blue glass indicates **K**
    - Place ¾ of the solution in a Marsh's apparatus, add pieces of zinc and a strip of platinum foil, when but little zinc remains heat 15 or 20 minutes, and throw contents of flask on a filter; wash thoroughly.
      - *Volatilized.* Collect spots on cold porcelain, and treat with NaClO. Spots dissolve; **As**. Spots do not dissolve; **Sb**. Test also with $AgNO_3$.
      - *Residue.* Treat with strong HNO_3, and filter.
        - *Residue.* Wash, boil with HCl and filter.
          - *Solution.* Put in a platinum dish with a piece of zinc. A dark spot on the platinum indicates **Sb**
          - *Residue.* Add to solution in platinum dish, boil with HCl, filter and add $HgCl_2$. *Precipitate* **Sn**
        - *Filtrate.* Divide into two parts.
          - *1st Half.* Add $SnCl_2$.
            - *Precipitate* **Hg**
          - *Second Half.* Add HCl, boil, then add excess of NaHO, wash the precipitate on filter with water, then with $(NH_4)HO$ containing NH_4Cl.
            - *Residue.* Dissolve on filter in very little HCl and add large quantity of H_2O to the filtrate. A cloudy precipitate indicates **Bi**
            - *Filtrate.* Divide into two parts.
              - *1st Half.* Acidify with HCl and Add $K_4Fe_2Cy_6$. *Precipitate* **Cu**
              - *2d Half.* Add excess of NaHO, a white gelatinous *Precipitate* **Cd**
      - *Filtrate.* Boil with a little HNO_3 and divide in two unequal parts.
        - *1st Portion.* Add KCyS. *Red Color* **Fe** *
        - *Second Portion.* Neutralize with $(NH_4)HO$, add excess of $Ba CO_3$, agitate ten minutes, filter and wash thoroughly.
          - *Precipitate.* Boil in a porcelain dish with dilute H_2SO_4 and filter. Add excess of NaHO to filtrate, a few drops of $KMnO_4$ and a little NH_4Cl. boil, filter, and divide the solution.
            - *1st Half.* Add some $H(C_2H_3O_2)$ and $Pb(C_2H_3O_2)_2$ *Precipitate* **Cr**
            - *2d Half.* Add excess of NH_4Cl *Precipitate* **Al**
          - *Filtrate.* Add excess of dilute H_2SO_4, filter, and saturate filtrate with $(NH_4)_2CO_3$, warm, filter, and wash.
            - *Precipitate.* Mix a portion with Na_2CO_3 and $NaNO_3$, fuse on platinum foil. *Green color.* **Mn**
            - Dissolve another portion in HCl, neutralize with $(NH_4)HO$, add considerable NH_4Cl and $(NH_4)_2C_2O_4$ *Precipitate* **Ca**
            - *Solution.* Add $Na_2 HPO_4$
              - *Precipitate* **Mg**
              - *Solution.* Evaporate to dryness, dissolve in HCl, add KNO_2 and $H(C_2H_3O_2)$, filter.
                - *Precipitate* **Co**
                - *Solution.* Add NaHO
                  - *Precipitate* **Ni**

* To determine degree of oxidation of Fe examine the original solution with $K_4Fe_2Cy_6$ and KCyS

N. B. To test for zinc mix a portion of the original solution with HCl, H_2SO_4, filter, add NaHO in excess, and boil. Add a little $(NH_4)_2CO_3$ and NH_4Cl to filtrate, boil until all odor of $(NH_4)HO$ is expelled, and filter. Add $K_4Fe_2Cy_6$ to solution, a cloud or precipitate indicates **Zn**.

In this scheme regard is had to the following substances in aqueous solution:—

I. PbO, Ag_2O, HgO
II. CaO, BaO, SrO
III. $(NH_4)_2O, Na_2O, K_2O$
IV. $As_2O_3, As_2O_5, Sb_2O_3, Sb_2O_5, SnO, SnO_2, Hg_2O, CuO, CdO, Bi_2O_3$
V. $FeO, Fe_2O_3, Cr_2O_3, Al_2O_3$
VI. MnO, MgO, CoO, NiO
VII. ZnO

INDEX.

LIST OF ADVERTISEMENTS

—OF—

ASSAYERS' SUPPLIES.

H. M. RAYNOR,

No. 25 Bond Street, New York.

PLATINUM.

SHEET AND WIRE, (Soft or Hard,) for all uses of Chemists, Dentists, Electro-Platers, Jewelers, Gunsmiths, Experimenters, &c., and for Telegraph Instruments, Batteries, Lightning-Rod Points, Gas Burners, &c.

BOILERS, (For Acid Works.)

ASSAYING APPARATUS

RETORTS AND STILLS,

CRUCIBLES, CAPSULES, DISHES.

TRIANGLES, SPATULAS,

BLOW-PIPE JETS AND SPOONS,

TWEEZERS & CRUCIBLE TONGS, (Platinum-Pointed.)

SCRAP CUTTINGS, for Solution, &c.

IRIDIUM AND PALLADIUM, to Order.

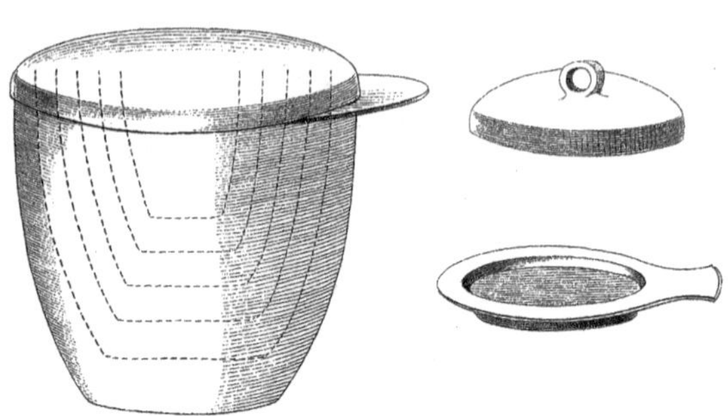

CRUCIBLES, Cost (approximate) according to weight,

CAPACITY.	
10 C. C. M.	$ 4.00
15 "	6,00
$22\frac{1}{2}$ "	8.00
30 "	11.50
50 "	14.50
75 "	19.00

Blowpipe Spoons.
$1,50 to $2.50

Boats,
$3.50 to $7.00.

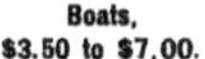

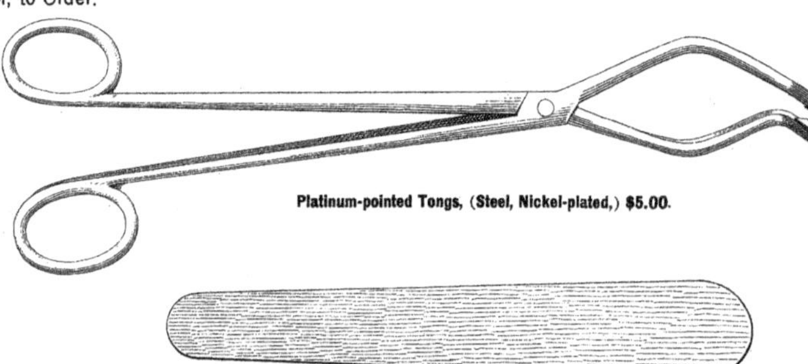

Platinum-pointed Tongs, (Steel, Nickel-plated,) $5.00.

Spatulas, from $1,50 (2 in. long,) upwards.

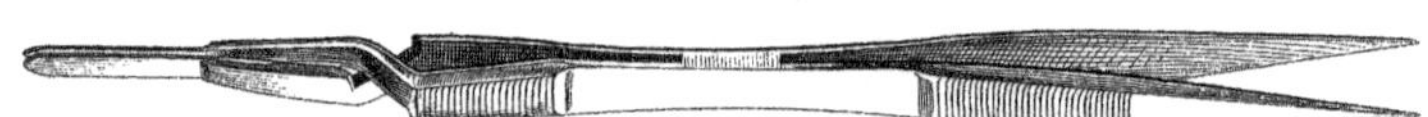

Platinum-pointed Forceps, (Steel, Nickel-plated,) $2,25.

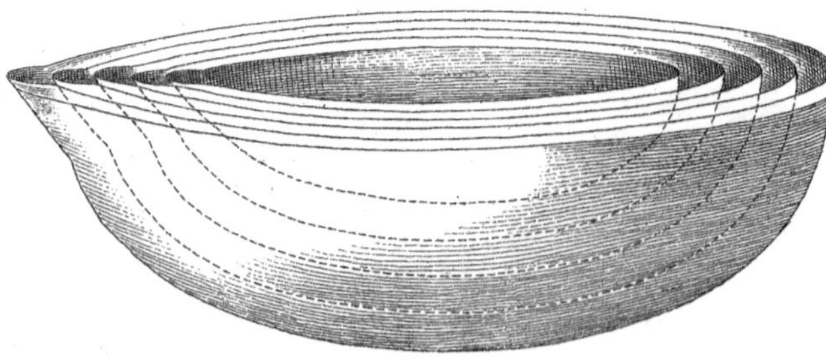

DISHES. Cost, (approximate) according to weight.

WIDTH.	
$1\frac{5}{8}$ in.	$ 5.00
2 "	7.50
$2\frac{1}{2}$ "	11.00
3 "	16.00
$3\frac{1}{4}$ "	21.00
$3\frac{1}{2}$ "	25.00
$4\frac{1}{2}$ "	33.00

BECKER & SONS,

MANUFACTURERS OF

Balances & Weights of Precision.

NO. 232 EAST 128th STREET, NEW YORK.

Every Balance and set of Weights leaving this establishment is guaranteed to be accurately adjusted as represented in our Price List, which can be had upon application.

Becker & Sons beg leave to state, that for some time past we have been aware that imitations of our Balances and Weights have been placed on the market, represented as being manufactured by us; and would caution our customers that only the goods made by us bear our firm name.

N. B.—We would also call attention to the fact that we have withdrawn our agency from Mr. E. B. Benjamin, who has acted as our agent for several years.

GEO. WALE & CO.,

Philosophical Instrument Makers to the Stevens Institute of Technology,

HOBOKEN, N. J.

Manufacture the COLLEGE LANTERN, for which they have received the SCOTT LEGACY PREMIUM of the FRANKLIN INSTITUTE, and the SILVER MEDAL OF THE AMERICAN INSTITUTE. See also Report of Committee of Science and Arts of Franklin Institute, Vol. LXX, p. 301, 1875.

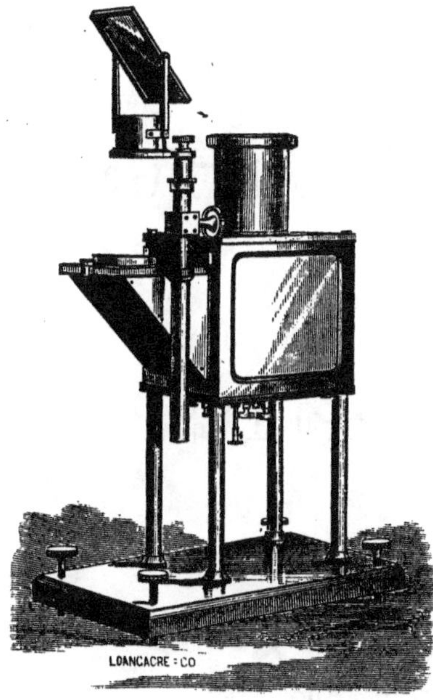

The following letter is only a specimen of numberless others of like substance which have been received from such gentlemen as Dr. CHANDLER, of New York, Prof. CROSS, of Boston, Dr. BARKER, of Philadelphia.

DEPARTMENT OF PHYSICS,
CORNELL UNIVERSITY,
ITHACA, N. Y., Feb. 11, 1875.

GENTLEMEN: As to your College Lantern, after using it *for three years*, I should only reiterate in stronger terms what I wrote after the first brief trial. Optically, it is all one could ask; mechanically, it is a fine piece of workmanship, and I have never seen its equal for the facility and celerity with which the various adjustments can be made. It works equally well as a vertical or horizontal lantern, except, of course, the necessary loss of light from reflection, and the change can be made from one to the other, as I have many times made it in the midst of a lecture, in less than half a minute. I receive many inquiries about lanterns, and I *always* refer them to you.

WILLIAM A. ANTHONY.

Microscopic and Polarizing Attachments, producing effects far surpassing anything before manufactured, are also on hand. Also, attachments for spectrum projections, for diffraction, Prof. Morton's Chromatrope, Eclipse Slide, &c., &c.

Also, manufacture the VERTICAL, the EXPERIMENTER'S and the PHOTOGRAPHER'S LANTERNS, together with MICROSCOPIC, POLARIZING, and various special attachments; SPECTROSCOPES of various forms.

Also, NON-RETREATING BUNSEN BURNERS, superior finish, 75 cents each; $6 per dozen. COPPER WATER-BATHS, extra heavy, 5½ inches diameter, $1.50 each; $15 per dozen. PLATNER'S BLOWPIPES AND APPARATUS of superior quality, nickel plated, at reduced rates. GLASS SLIDES AND PHILOSOPHICAL APPARATUS generally, at low rates.

ILLUSTRATED PRICE LISTS SENT ON APPLICATION.

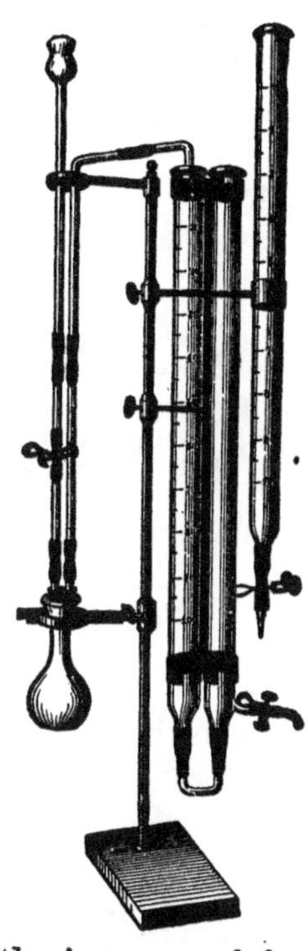

Rohrbeck & Goebeler,

NO. 4 MURRAY ST., NEW YORK.

Importers and Manufacturers of

Chemical & Physical Apparatus,

INSTRUMENTS, UTENSILS,

and Materials for Metallurgical Assaying, for the Cupellation of Gold and Silver, and for Mineralogical Determination.

Also Dealers in

MINERALS, PURE CHEMICALS and REAGENTS,

inform their customers that their stock of the above articles has been lately completed to a great extent by new importations of partly new apparatus, and by the increase of facilities in the manufacture of those goods here and in Europe, so that they will be prepared to fill orders without delay, and to furnish first-class articles at prices lower than other dealers.

ROHRBECK & GOEBELER also beg to inform their friends that Doctor W. I. ROHRBECK, of Berlin, has lately entered personally into the firm, of which until now he was a silent partner, and that in connection with Doctor J. FETTBACK, also of Berlin, he will superintend the scientific and illustrative branches of the business, which otherwise will be conducted on the same principles, and with the same care in the speedy and conscientious execution of orders as in former years.

Catalogues will be mailed on application without charge.

www.ingramcontent.com/pod-product-compliance
Lightning Source LLC
LaVergne TN
LVHW011219110826
845150LV00006B/1480

* 9 7 8 1 4 2 5 5 1 6 6 7 3 *